Python for Cryptocurrency Trading

Navigate the Digital Currency Market

J.P.Morgan

DISCOVER OTHER BOOKS IN THE SERIES 6

DISCLAIMER 8

INTRODUCTION 9

CHAPTER 1: CRYPTOCURRENCY TRADING WITH PYTHON
.... 11

THE IMPORTANCE OF CRYPTOCURRENCY IN MODERN FINANCE............14
THE POWER OF PYTHON FOR CRYPTOCURRENCY TRADING 17

CHAPTER 2: GETTING STARTED WITH PYTHON FOR
FINANCE 19

SETTING UP YOUR PYTHON ENVIRONMENT 23
ESSENTIAL PYTHON LIBRARIES FOR FINANCE............................27

CHAPTER 3: UNDERSTANDING THE CRYPTOCURRENCY
MARKET 30

KEY CONCEPTS IN CRYPTOCURRENCY TRADING............................34
THE VOLATILITY AND RISKS OF DIGITAL CURRENCIES.............................39

CHAPTER 4 :ANALYZING BLOCKCHAIN DATA WITH
PYTHON 43

INTRODUCTION TO BLOCKCHAIN TECHNOLOGY............................47
ACCESSING AND ANALYZING BLOCKCHAIN DATA WITH PYTHON - SCRIPTS
.... 50

CHAPTER 5: CRYPTOCURRENCY MARKET DATA
SOURCES 55

POPULAR CRYPTOCURRENCY EXCHANGES.....................................59
ACCESSING MARKET DATA VIA APIS WITH PYTHON - SCRIPTS 63

CHAPTER 6: TECHNICAL ANALYSIS FOR
CRYPTOCURRENCY TRADING 68

TECHNICAL ANALYSIS IN CRYPTOCURRENCY TRADING...............................73
IMPLEMENTING TECHNICAL INDICATORS IN PYTHON WITH PYTHON -
SCRIPTS..76

CHAPTER 7: DEVELOPING TRADING BOTS WITH PYTHON

....81

INTRODUCTION TO TRADING BOTS..86
BUILDING YOUR FIRST TRADING BOT WITH PYTHON - SCRIPTS...............89

CHAPTER 8: BACKTESTING TRADING STRATEGIES 93

IMPORTANCE OF BACKTESTING TRADING STRATEGIES............................96
IMPLEMENTING BACKTESTING IN PYTHON - SCRIPTS................................99

CHAPTER 9: MACHINE LEARNING FOR PREDICTIVE
TRADING 104

INTRODUCTION TO MACHINE LEARNING IN FINANCE 106
USING MACHINE LEARNING ALGORITHMS FOR TRADING PREDICTIONS
WITH PYTHON... 110

CHAPTER 10: SENTIMENT ANALYSIS FOR
CRYPTOCURRENCY MARKETS 115

UNDERSTANDING SENTIMENT ANALYSIS IN CRYPTOCURRENCY MARKETS
.... 118
IMPLEMENTING SENTIMENT ANALYSIS WITH PYTHON - SCRIPTS......... 121

CHAPTER 11: ALGORITHMIC TRADING STRATEGIES 126

ALGORITHMIC TRADING FUNDAMENTALS... 129
DEVELOPING AND TESTING ALGORITHMIC STRATEGIES......................... 132

CHAPTER 12: RISK MANAGEMENT IN CRYPTOCURRENCY
TRADING 135

UNDERSTANDING RISK IN TRADING.. 138
IMPLEMENTING RISK MANAGEMENT TECHNIQUES WITH PYTHON -
SCRIPTS... 141

CHAPTER 13: PORTFOLIO MANAGEMENT AND
DIVERSIFICATION 145

PORTFOLIO MANAGEMENT MARKET MAKING IN TRADING 148
STRATEGIES FOR DIVERSIFYING CRYPTOCURRENCY INVESTMENTS...... 151

CHAPTER 14: CRYPTOCURRENCY ARBITRAGE
OPPORTUNITIES 156

UNDERSTANDING ARBITRAGE IN CRYPTOCURRENCY MARKETS............ 159
IMPLEMENTING ARBITRAGE STRATEGIES WITH PYTHON SCRIPTS......... 162

CHAPTER 15: ADVANCED TRADING BOT DEVELOPMENT
.... **166**

ENHANCING YOUR TRADING BOT.. 169
USING AI AND ML TO IMPROVE BOT PERFORMANCE WITH PYTHON -
SCRIPTS.. 174

CHAPTER 16: HIGH-FREQUENCY TRADING (HFT) IN CRYPTOCURRENCIES.. **179**

INTRODUCTION TO FREQUENCY TRADING HFT 182
IMPLEMENTING HFT STRATEGIES WITH PYTHON SCRIPTS.................... 184

CHAPTER 17: REGULATIONS AND COMPLIANCE IN CRYPTOCURRENCY TRADING **189**

UNDERSTANDING REGULATORY CHALLENGES IN CRYPTOCURRENCY
TRADING 192
STAYING COMPLIANT IN THE CRYPTOCURRENCY MARKET 196

CHAPTER 18: SECURITY AND PRIVACY IN CRYPTOCURRENCY TRADING **199**

SECURING YOUR TRADING ENVIRONMENT WITH PYTHON - SCRIPTS.... 202
PROTECTING YOUR DIGITAL ASSETS WITH PYTHON - SCRIPTS............... 205

CHAPTER 19: DEVELOPING CUSTOM TRADING INDICATORS **209**

CUSTOM INDICATORS FOR EXCHANGES IN TRADING WITH PYTHON -
SCRIPTS.. 214
IMPLEMENTING CUSTOM INDICATORS IN PYTHON SCRIPTS.................... 218

CHAPTER 20: INTEGRATING TRADING BOTS WITH EXCHANGES.. **223**

API INTEGRATION WITH EXCHANGES WITH PYTHON - SCRIPTS............. 226
AUTOMATING TRADING PROCESSES WITH PYTHON - SCRIPTS 230

CHAPTER 21: TRADING PSYCHOLOGY AND DISCIPLINE
.... **235**

UNDERSTANDING TRADING PSYCHOLOGY 238
TECHNIQUES FOR MAINTAINING DISCIPLINE TRADING PSYCHOLOGY.. 241

CHAPTER 22: REAL-TIME DATA PROCESSING AND ANALYSIS 244

HANDLING REAL-TIME DATA IN PYTHON - SCRIPTS 248
ANALYZING REAL-TIME MARKET TRENDS WITH PYTHON - SCRIPTS..... 253

CONCLUSION 258

BIOGRAPHY 260

GLOSSARY: PYTHON FOR CRYPTOCURRENCY TRADING
.... 262

Discover Other Books in the Series

"Python for Algorithmic Trading: Mastering Strategies for Consistent Profits"

"Python for Automated Trading Systems: Building Your Own Bots for Stock and Crypto Markets"

"Python for Financial Data Analysis: Unlock the Secrets of the Market"

"Python for Predictive Analytics in Finance: Anticipate Market Movements"

Disclaimer

The information provided in this book, *Python for Cryptocurrency Trading: Navigate the Digital Currency Market*, by J.P. Morgan, is for educational and informational purposes only. The content of this book is designed to provide insights into cryptocurrency trading using Python and to guide readers in developing their own trading strategies and tools.

The author is not a licensed financial advisor, and the information contained in this book should not be construed as such. Readers are encouraged to seek professional advice before making any financial decisions or engaging in cryptocurrency trading.

While every effort has been made to ensure the accuracy and reliability of the information presented, the author makes no representations or warranties regarding the completeness, accuracy, or suitability of the content. Cryptocurrency markets are highly volatile and unpredictable; past performance is not indicative of future results.

Introduction

Welcome to *"**Python for Cryptocurrency Trading: Navigate the Digital Currency Market**"*. In the rapidly evolving world of finance, cryptocurrencies have emerged as a revolutionary force, offering unparalleled opportunities for savvy traders. Whether you're a seasoned Python programmer, a web development enthusiast, a budding trader, or a student eager to explore the intersection of technology and finance, this book is your gateway to mastering cryptocurrency trading through the power of Python.

The allure of cryptocurrencies lies in their potential for high returns and the excitement of navigating an ever-changing market. However, with great opportunity comes great complexity. This is where Python, with its simplicity and versatility, becomes an indispensable tool. By combining Python's robust capabilities with the intricacies of the cryptocurrency market, you can develop sophisticated trading bots, analyze vast amounts of blockchain data, and implement effective trading strategies that will set you apart from the crowd.

In this book, we will embark on a journey that covers everything you need to know to thrive in the digital currency market. We will start by laying a strong foundation, delving into the fundamentals of cryptocurrencies and the blockchain technology that powers them. From there, we'll guide you through the essentials of Python programming, ensuring you have the skills to tackle more advanced topics with confidence.

Next, we'll explore the exciting world of trading bots. You'll learn how to design, build, and optimize bots that can execute trades with precision and speed, leveraging real-time data to make informed decisions. Our deep dive into blockchain data analysis will equip you with the tools to extract valuable insights from the seemingly chaotic world of digital transactions, enabling you to stay ahead of market trends.

Chapter 1: Cryptocurrency Trading with Python

Cryptocurrency trading has become a popular way for individuals to invest in digital assets and potentially earn profits. With the rise of cryptocurrencies such as Bitcoin, Ethereum, and Litecoin, more and more people are looking to get involved in this exciting market.

One of the key tools that traders use to analyze and execute trades in the cryptocurrency market is Python. Python is a versatile and powerful programming language that is widely used in the financial industry for data analysis, algorithmic trading, and automation of trading strategies.

In this chapter, we will introduce you to the basics of cryptocurrency trading with Python. We will cover the fundamental concepts of cryptocurrency trading, explain how Python can be used to analyze and trade cryptocurrencies, and provide you with the necessary tools and resources to get started.

Cryptocurrency trading involves buying and selling digital assets on various cryptocurrency exchanges. These exchanges allow users to trade cryptocurrencies against other digital assets or fiat currencies such as the US dollar or the Euro. Traders can profit from price movements in the cryptocurrency market by buying low and selling high, or by shorting cryptocurrencies and profiting from price declines.

Python is a popular programming language among cryptocurrency traders because of its simplicity, flexibility, and extensive libraries for data analysis and visualization. Python can be used to access market data from cryptocurrency exchanges, perform technical analysis on price data, backtest trading strategies, and automate the execution of trades.

To get started with cryptocurrency trading in Python, you will need to install the necessary libraries and tools. Some of the most popular libraries for cryptocurrency trading in Python include ccxt, pandas, numpy, matplotlib, and talib. These libraries provide functions for accessing market data from cryptocurrency exchanges, performing technical analysis on price data, and visualizing trading signals.

Once you have installed the necessary libraries, you can start writing Python scripts to analyze and trade cryptocurrencies. For example, you can use the ccxt library to connect to a cryptocurrency exchange, retrieve market data for a specific cryptocurrency pair, and plot the price data using matplotlib. You can also use the pandas library to calculate technical indicators such as moving averages, relative strength index (RSI), and MACD.

In addition to analyzing market data, Python can also be used to backtest trading strategies and automate the execution of trades. Backtesting involves testing a trading strategy on historical data to evaluate its performance and profitability. Python provides libraries such as backtrader and zipline for backtesting trading strategies and simulating trades in a historical market environment.

Automating the execution of trades in Python involves connecting to a cryptocurrency exchange via an API, placing buy and sell orders based on predefined trading signals, and monitoring the performance of the trading strategy. Python provides libraries such as ccxt and requests for interacting with cryptocurrency exchanges via their APIs and executing trades programmatically.

In this chapter, we have introduced you to the basics of cryptocurrency trading with Python. We have explained how Python can be used to analyze market data, backtest trading strategies, and automate the execution of trades in the cryptocurrency market. We have also provided you with the necessary tools and resources to get started with cryptocurrency trading in Python.

In the next chapter, we will dive deeper into the technical aspects of cryptocurrency trading with Python. We will cover topics such as accessing market data from cryptocurrency exchanges, performing technical analysis on price data, backtesting trading strategies, and automating the execution of trades. By the end of this book, you will have the knowledge and skills to become a successful cryptocurrency trader using Python.

The Importance of Cryptocurrency in Modern Finance

Cryptocurrency has become a hot topic in the world of finance in recent years, with many people investing in digital assets like Bitcoin, Ethereum, and Litecoin. But what exactly is cryptocurrency, and why is it so important in modern finance?

Cryptocurrency is a form of digital currency that uses cryptography to secure transactions, control the creation of new units, and verify the transfer of assets. Unlike traditional currencies issued by governments, cryptocurrencies are decentralized and operate on a technology called blockchain. This technology allows for secure, transparent, and immutable transactions without the need for intermediaries like banks or financial institutions.

One of the key reasons why cryptocurrency is important in modern finance is its potential to revolutionize the way we think about money. With traditional currencies, transactions are often slow, expensive, and subject to government regulations. Cryptocurrencies, on the other hand, offer a faster, cheaper, and more efficient way to transfer value across borders and between individuals.

For example, sending money overseas using traditional banking methods can be costly and time-consuming, with fees and exchange rates eating into the amount being transferred. With cryptocurrencies, transactions can be completed in minutes and at a fraction of the cost, making it an attractive option for people looking to send money internationally.

Another important aspect of cryptocurrency is its potential to provide financial inclusion to people who are underserved by traditional banking systems. According to the World Bank, around 1.7 billion adults worldwide do not have access to a bank account, making it difficult for them to save, borrow, or invest money.
Cryptocurrencies offer a way for these individuals to participate in the global economy without the need for a traditional bank account.

In addition to providing financial inclusion, cryptocurrencies also offer a level of privacy and security that is unmatched by traditional banking systems. With traditional banks, transactions are recorded and stored in centralized databases, making them vulnerable to hacking and fraud. Cryptocurrencies, on the other hand, use advanced encryption techniques to secure transactions and protect user data, making them a more secure option for storing and transferring value.

Cryptocurrency also has the potential to disrupt traditional financial systems by offering an alternative to central banks and fiat currencies. Central banks have the power to print money and manipulate interest rates, which can lead to inflation and economic instability. Cryptocurrencies, on the other hand, have a fixed supply and are not controlled by any single entity, making them immune to government interference and inflation.

One of the most popular cryptocurrencies, Bitcoin, was

created in 2009 as a response to the global financial crisis and the perceived failures of traditional banking systems. Since then, Bitcoin has grown in popularity and value, with many people viewing it as a safe haven asset and a hedge against inflation.

In addition to Bitcoin, there are thousands of other cryptocurrencies in existence, each with its own unique features and use cases. Ethereum, for example, is a cryptocurrency that also serves as a platform for decentralized applications and smart contracts. Litecoin is another popular cryptocurrency that offers faster transaction speeds and lower fees than Bitcoin.

Overall, the importance of cryptocurrency in modern finance cannot be understated. From providing financial inclusion to offering privacy and security, cryptocurrencies have the potential to revolutionize the way we think about money and banking. As the technology continues to evolve and gain mainstream acceptance, it will be interesting to see how cryptocurrencies shape the future of finance.

The Power of Python for Cryptocurrency Trading

Python has become a popular programming language in the world of cryptocurrency trading due to its versatility, ease of use, and powerful libraries. With its simple syntax and extensive libraries, Python has become the go-to language for traders looking to automate their trading strategies, analyze market data, and create custom indicators.

One of the key reasons why Python is so powerful for cryptocurrency trading is its extensive library support. Libraries such as Pandas, NumPy, and Matplotlib make it easy to analyze and visualize market data, while libraries like ccxt and pyalgotrade provide tools for interacting with cryptocurrency exchanges and implementing trading strategies.

Pandas is a powerful data manipulation library that allows traders to easily manipulate and analyze large datasets. With Pandas, traders can quickly load market data into a DataFrame, perform calculations on the data, and create custom indicators to inform their trading decisions.

NumPy is another essential library for cryptocurrency traders, as it provides support for numerical operations and mathematical functions. Traders can use NumPy to perform complex calculations on market data, such as calculating moving averages, standard deviations, and other statistical measures.

Matplotlib is a popular library for creating visualizations of market data. Traders can use Matplotlib to create line charts, candlestick charts, and other visualizations to gain insights into market trends and patterns.

In addition to these libraries, Python also has a wide range of libraries for interacting with cryptocurrency exchanges. The ccxt library, for example, provides a unified API for interacting with over 100 cryptocurrency exchanges, making it easy for traders to automate their trading strategies across multiple exchanges.

Another powerful library for cryptocurrency trading is pyalgotrade, which provides tools for backtesting trading strategies and implementing algorithmic trading systems. With pyalgotrade, traders can test their strategies against historical market data to see how they would have performed in the past, and then deploy them in real-time trading.

Python's simplicity and readability also make it an ideal language for traders looking to quickly prototype and test new trading strategies. With its clean syntax and extensive library support, traders can quickly implement and test new ideas without getting bogged down in complex code.

Overall, the power of Python for cryptocurrency trading lies in its versatility, ease of use, and extensive library support. Whether you're a beginner looking to automate simple trading strategies or an experienced trader looking to implement complex algorithmic systems, Python has the tools and libraries you need to succeed in the world of cryptocurrency trading.

Chapter 2: Getting Started with Python for Finance

In today's fast-paced world, technology plays a crucial role in almost every aspect of our lives. This is especially true in the finance industry, where the use of technology has revolutionized the way financial professionals analyze data, make decisions, and manage risk. One of the most popular programming languages used in finance is Python. Python is a versatile and powerful language that is well-suited for financial analysis, modeling, and automation. In this chapter, we will explore how to get started with Python for finance and the key concepts you need to understand to leverage Python effectively in the finance industry.

Why Python for Finance?

Python has gained popularity in the finance industry for several reasons. First and foremost, Python is a versatile language that is easy to learn and use. Its simple syntax and readability make it an ideal choice for financial professionals who may not have a background in computer science. Additionally, Python has a robust ecosystem of libraries and tools that are specifically designed for financial analysis and modeling. These libraries, such as Pandas, NumPy, and Matplotlib, make it easy to work with financial data, perform complex calculations, and visualize results.

Another key advantage of Python is its flexibility and

scalability. Python can be used for a wide range of tasks in finance, from data analysis and visualization to building complex financial models and algorithms. Its scalability makes it suitable for both small-scale projects and large-scale applications. Additionally, Python is an open-source language, which means that there is a vast community of developers who contribute to its development and provide support through forums, tutorials, and online resources.

Getting Started with Python

To get started with Python for finance, you will need to install Python on your computer. Python is available for download from the official website (www.python.org) and is compatible with Windows, Mac, and Linux operating systems. Once you have installed Python, you can start writing and running Python code using an integrated development environment (IDE) such as PyCharm, Jupyter Notebook, or Spyder.

Before diving into financial analysis with Python, it is important to understand some key concepts of the language. Python is an object-oriented programming language, which means that it organizes code into objects that contain data and methods. Objects are instances of classes, which are blueprints for creating objects with specific attributes and behaviors. In Python, everything is an object, including integers, strings, lists, and dictionaries.

Python also supports a wide range of data types, including integers, floats, strings, lists, tuples, sets, and dictionaries. Understanding these data types is essential for working with financial data and performing calculations. For example, you can use lists to store a series of values, such as stock prices or trading volumes,and dictionaries to store key-value pairs, such as stock symbols and company names.

Working with Financial Data

One of the key tasks in finance is working with financial data, such as stock prices, market indices, and economic indicators. Python provides several libraries that make it easy to import, manipulate, and analyze financial data. One of the most popular libraries for working with financial data is Pandas. Pandas is a powerful data manipulation library that provides data structures and functions for working with structured data, such as time series and panel data.

To start working with financial data in Python, you first need to import the Pandas library. You can do this byusing the import statement followed by the library name:

import pandas as pd

This statement imports the Pandas library and assigns it an alias, pd, which makes it easier to reference the library in your code. Once you have imported the Pandas library, you can use its functions and data structures to read, manipulate, and analyze financial data.

For example, you can use the read_csv function to import a CSV file containing historical stock prices into aPandas DataFrame:

```
df = pd.read_csv('stock_prices.csv')
```

This statement reads the CSV file 'stock_prices.csv' and stores the data in a Pandas DataFrame called df. You can then use the DataFrame to perform various operations on the data, such as calculating returns, analyzing trends, and visualizing results.

We have explored the key concepts of Python for finance and how to get started with working with financial data in Python. Python is a versatile and powerful language that is well-suited for financial analysis, modeling, and automation.

By understanding the fundamentals of Python and its libraries, such as Pandas, NumPy, and Matplotlib, you can leverage Python effectively in the finance industry to make informed decisions, manage risk, and drive business growth. In the next chapter, we will delve deeper into financial modeling with Python and explore how to build and analyze financial models using Python.

Setting Up Your Python Environment

Python is a powerful and versatile programming language that is widely used in various fields such as web development, data science, machine learning, and automation. Setting up your Python environment is the first step towards working with this language efficiently and effectively. In this article, we will guide you through the process of setting up your Python environment on your computer.

Step 1: Download Python

The first step in setting up your Python environment is to download the Python interpreter. You can download the latest version of Python from the official Python website (https://www.python.org/). Python is available for Windows, macOS, and Linux operating systems, so make sure to download the version that is compatible with your operating system.

Once you have downloaded the Python installer, run the installer and follow the on-screen instructions to install Python on your computer. During the installation process, make sure to check the box that says "Add Python to PATH" so that you can easily run Python from the command line.

Step 2: Install a Code Editor

While you can write Python code in any text editor, using a code editor specifically designed for programming can

23

make your coding experience much smoother. Some popular code editors for Python include Visual Studio Code, PyCharm, and Sublime Text.

You can download and install any of these code editors from their respective websites. Once you have installed a code editor, you can open it and start writing Python code.

Step 3: Install Package Manager

Python has a vast ecosystem of libraries and packages that you can use to extend the functionality of the language. To manage these packages, you can use a package manager such as pip. Pip is the default package manager for Python, and it allows you to easily install, upgrade, and remove Python packages.

To install pip, open a command prompt or terminal window and run the following command:

```
python -m ensurepip
```

This command will install pip on your system. You can then use pip to install any Python packages that you need for your projects.

Step 4: Create a Virtual Environment

A virtual environment is a self-contained directory that contains a specific version of Python and all the packages that you need for a particular project. Using virtual environments can help you avoid conflicts between different projects that require different versions of Python or different packages.

To create a virtual environment, open a command prompt or terminal window and run the following command:

```
` ` `

python -m venv myenv
` ` `
```

This command will create a new virtual environment called "myenv" in the current directory. You can activate the virtual environment by running the following command:

On Windows:
```
` ` ` myenv\Scripts\activate
` ` `
```

On macOS and Linux:
```
` ` `

source myenv/bin/activate
` ` `
```

Once the virtual environment is activated, you can install any packages that you need for your project using pip. When you are done working on your project, you can deactivate the virtual environment by running the command "deactivate".

Step 5: Start Coding

Now that you have set up your Python environment, you

can start writing Python code in your code editor. You can create a new Python file, write your code, and save the file with a .py extension.

To run your Python code, open a command prompt or terminal window, navigate to the directory where your Python file is located, and run the following command:

```
python filename.py
```

This command will run your Python code and display the output in the command prompt or terminal window.
Conclusion
Setting up your Python environment is the first step towards becoming proficient in the Python programming language. By following the steps outlined in this article, you can create a Python environment on your computer and start writing Python code for your projects. Remember to regularly update your Python interpreter and packages to ensure that you are using the latest features and improvements in the language. Happy coding!

Essential Python Libraries for Finance

Python has become one of the most popular programming languages in the financial industry due to its flexibility, ease of use, and extensive library support. In this article, we will explore some of the essential Pythonlibraries that are commonly used in finance.

NumPy: NumPy is a fundamental library for scientific computing in Python. It provides support for large, multi-dimensional arrays and matrices, along with a collection of mathematical functions to operate on these arrays. In finance, NumPy is commonly used for data manipulation, numerical analysis, and statistical calculations.

Pandas: Pandas is a powerful data manipulation library built on top of NumPy. It provides data structures like Series and DataFrame that make it easy to work with structured data. In finance, Pandas is widely used for data analysis, data cleaning, and data visualization.

Matplotlib: Matplotlib is a plotting library for creating static, animated, and interactive visualizations in Python. It provides a wide range of plotting functions to create line plots, bar plots, scatter plots, histograms, and more. In finance, Matplotlib is often used to visualize stock price movements, portfolio performance, and other financial data.

Seaborn: Seaborn is a statistical data visualization library based on Matplotlib. It provides a high-level interface for creating attractive and informative statistical graphics.

Seaborn is commonly used in finance for creating visually appealing plots and charts that help in understanding complex financial data.

Scikit-learn: Scikit-learn is a machine learning library for Python that provides a wide range of supervised and unsupervised learning algorithms. In finance, Scikit-learn is used for tasks like stock price prediction, risk assessment, fraud detection, and portfolio optimization.

TensorFlow: TensorFlow is an open-source machine learning library developed by Google. It provides tools for building and training deep learning models, including neural networks, convolutional neural networks, and recurrent neural networks. In finance, TensorFlow is used for tasks like algorithmic trading, sentiment analysis, and credit risk modeling.

Statsmodels: Statsmodels is a statistical modeling library for Python that provides tools for estimating and interpreting statistical models. It includes a wide range of statistical tests, regression models, time series analysis, and more. In finance, Statsmodels is commonly used for analyzing financial data, building econometric models, and conducting hypothesis testing.

Quantlib: Quantlib is a quantitative finance library for modeling, trading, and risk management. It provides tools for pricing derivatives, calculating risk metrics, and simulating financial markets. Quantlib is widely used in the finance industry for tasks like valuing options, pricing bonds, and managing financial risk.

Pyfolio: Pyfolio is a performance and risk analysis library for financial portfolios. It provides tools for analyzing portfolio returns, risk metrics, and performance attribution. Pyfolio is commonly used by quantitative analysts, portfolio managers, and risk managers to evaluate the performance of investment strategies.

Zipline: Zipline is a backtesting and live trading engine for algorithmic trading strategies. It provides tools for developing, testing, and deploying trading algorithms in Python. Zipline is used by quantitative traders, hedge funds, and financial institutions to backtest and optimize trading strategies before deploying them in live markets.

Python has a rich ecosystem of libraries that make it an ideal programming language for finance. Whether you are analyzing financial data, building machine learning models, or developing trading strategies, there is a Python library to support your needs. By leveraging these essential Python libraries, finance professionals can gain valuable insights, make informed decisions, and stay ahead in today's competitive financial markets.

Chapter 3: Understanding the Cryptocurrency Market

The cryptocurrency market is a fast-paced and ever-changing landscape that can be both exciting and overwhelming for newcomers. In this chapter, we will delve into the key aspects of the cryptocurrency market, including its history, major players, and factors that influence its volatility.

History of the Cryptocurrency Market

The cryptocurrency market was born in 2009 with the creation of Bitcoin by an unknown person or group of people using the pseudonym Satoshi Nakamoto. Bitcoin was the first decentralized digital currency, meaning that it operates without a central authority like a government or bank. This revolutionary concept sparked the creation of thousands of other cryptocurrencies, each with its own unique features and use cases.

Over the years, the cryptocurrency market has experienced significant growth and evolution. In the early days, Bitcoin was primarily used for online transactions and as a store of value. However, as more people became interested in cryptocurrencies, new use cases emerged, such as decentralized finance (DeFi), non-fungible tokens (NFTs), and smart contracts.

Major Players in the Cryptocurrency Market

The cryptocurrency market is made up of a diverse range of participants, each playing a unique role in shaping its dynamics. Some of the major players in the cryptocurrency market include:

Investors: Individuals and institutions who buy and hold cryptocurrencies as a long-term investment or for trading purposes.

Miners: Individuals or groups who use powerful computers to solve complex mathematical puzzles and validate transactions on the blockchain in exchange for newly minted coins.

Exchanges: Platforms that facilitate the buying, selling, and trading of cryptocurrencies. Some of the most popular cryptocurrency exchanges include Coinbase, Binance, and Kraken.

Developers: Individuals or teams who create and maintain the code for different cryptocurrencies and blockchain projects.

Regulators: Government agencies and regulatory bodies that oversee the cryptocurrency market and enforce laws and regulations to protect investors and prevent fraud.

Factors Influencing Cryptocurrency Volatility

The cryptocurrency market is known for its high volatility, with prices often experiencing sharp fluctuations in a short period of time. There are several factors that can influence the volatility of cryptocurrencies, including:

31

Market Sentiment: The overall mood of the market can have a significant impact on cryptocurrency prices. Positive news, such as the adoption of cryptocurrencies by major companies or governments, can drive prices higher, while negative news, such as regulatory crackdowns or security breaches, can cause prices to plummet.

Supply and Demand: Like any other asset, the price of a cryptocurrency is determined by supply and demand. If there is a high demand for a particular cryptocurrency and a limited supply, prices are likely to rise. Conversely, if there is a low demand and a high supply, prices may fall.

Regulatory Environment: Regulations play a crucial role in shaping the cryptocurrency market. Changes in regulations can have a direct impact on the price of cryptocurrencies, as investors may react to new laws or restrictions by buying or selling their holdings.

Technological Developments: Advances in blockchain technology and new features or upgrades to existing cryptocurrencies can also influence their prices. For example, the launch of a new decentralized application (dApp) or a major software update can attract more users and investors, leading to a price increase.

Market Manipulation: The cryptocurrency market is susceptible to manipulation by large investors or groups who have the power to influence prices through coordinated buying or selling. This can create artificial price movements that may not reflect the true value of a cryptocurrency.

The cryptocurrency market is a dynamic and complex ecosystem that is constantly evolving. By understanding the history, major players, and factors that influence its volatility, investors can make more informed decisions and navigate the market with confidence. In the next chapter, we will explore different investment strategies for profiting from the cryptocurrency market.

Key Concepts in Cryptocurrency Trading

Cryptocurrency trading is a rapidly growing market that has gained popularity in recent years. With the rise of digital currencies like Bitcoin, Ethereum, and many others, more and more people are getting involved in trading these assets. However, cryptocurrency trading can be complex and risky, especially for beginners. In this article, we will explore some key concepts in cryptocurrency trading to help you understand the basics and make informed decisions when investing in this market.

What is Cryptocurrency Trading?

Cryptocurrency trading is the act of buying and selling digital currencies on various online platforms. Unlike traditional financial markets, cryptocurrency trading operates 24/7, allowing traders to buy and sell assets at any time of the day or night. The goal of cryptocurrency trading is to profit from the price movements of digital currencies by buying low and selling high.

Types of Cryptocurrency Trading

There are several types of cryptocurrency trading, each with its unique characteristics and risks. The most common types of cryptocurrency trading include:

Day Trading: Day traders buy and sell digital currencies within a single day, taking advantage of short-term price fluctuations to make quick profits.

Swing Trading: Swing traders hold onto digital currencies for a few days or weeks, aiming to profit from medium-term price trends.

Scalping: Scalpers make small profits by buying and selling digital currencies quickly, often within minutes or seconds.

HODLing: HODLers hold onto digital currencies for the long term, believing in the potential growth of the assets over time.

Key Concepts in Cryptocurrency Trading

To be successful in cryptocurrency trading, it is essential to understand some key concepts that can help you make informed decisions and manage risks effectively. Some of the most important concepts in cryptocurrency trading include:

Market Analysis: Market analysis involves studying the price movements of digital currencies to identify trends and patterns that can help predict future price movements. There are two main types of market analysis: technical analysis and fundamental analysis.

Technical Analysis: Technical analysis involves analyzing historical price data and using various indicators and chart patterns to predict future price movements. Traders use tools like moving averages, RSI, MACD, and Fibonacci retracement levels to make informed trading decisions.

Fundamental Analysis: Fundamental analysis involves evaluating the underlying factors that can affect the value of digital currencies, such as news, events, regulations, and market sentiment. Traders use fundamental analysis to assess the long-term potential of digital currencies and make investment decisions based on their findings.

Risk Management: Risk management is a crucial concept in cryptocurrency trading, as the market is highly volatile and unpredictable. Traders should set stop-loss orders, diversify their portfolios, and only invest money they can afford to lose to minimize risks and protect their capital.

Trading Strategies: There are various trading strategies that traders can use to profit from cryptocurrency trading, such as trend following, range trading, breakout trading, and arbitrage. Each strategy has its pros and cons, so it is essential to choose the one that best suits your trading style and risk tolerance.

Wallet Security: Cryptocurrency trading involves storing digital assets in online wallets, which can be vulnerable to hacking and theft. Traders should use secure wallets, enable two-factor authentication, and store their private keys offline to protect their funds from unauthorized access.

Regulation: Cryptocurrency trading is a relatively new and unregulated market, which can expose traders to risks like fraud, scams, and market manipulation. It is essential to research the regulations in your country and choose reputable exchanges that comply with industry standards to ensure the safety of your investments.

Common Mistakes in Cryptocurrency Trading

While cryptocurrency trading can be profitable, many traders make common mistakes that can result in losses and missed opportunities. Some of the most common mistakes in cryptocurrency trading include:

FOMO (Fear of Missing Out): FOMO is a common phenomenon in cryptocurrency trading, where traders buy assets at inflated prices due to the fear of missing out on potential profits. This can lead to losses when the price of the asset corrects.

Overtrading: Overtrading is another common mistake in cryptocurrency trading, where traders make too many trades in a short period, leading to higher transaction costs and increased risks. It is essential to trade strategically and only take positions when there is a clear opportunity.

Ignoring Risk Management: Risk management is crucial in cryptocurrency trading, as the market is highly volatile and unpredictable. Traders should set stop-loss orders, diversify their portfolios, and avoid investing more than they can afford to lose to protect their capital.

Lack of Research: Many traders fail to conduct proper research before investing in digital currencies, leading to poor investment decisions and missed opportunities. It is essential to stay informed about market trends, news, and events that can affect the value of digital currencies.

Emotional Trading: Emotional trading is a common mistake in cryptocurrency trading, where traders make decisions based on fear, greed, or other emotions rather than logic and analysis.

The Volatility and Risks of Digital Currencies

The world of digital currencies, also known as cryptocurrencies, has been a hot topic in recent years. With the rise of Bitcoin and other digital currencies, many people have been drawn to the potential for high returns and the promise of a decentralized financial system. However, with this potential for high rewards also comes high risks and volatility.

One of the key characteristics of digital currencies is their volatility. Unlike traditional currencies, which are backed by governments and central banks, digital currencies are decentralized and their value is determined by supply and demand. This means that the value of digital currencies can fluctuate wildly in a short period of time.

For example, Bitcoin, the most well-known digital currency, has seen its value soar from just a few cents to over
$60,000 in the span of a few years. However, it has also experienced sharp drops in value, with prices falling by over 80% in some cases. This volatility can make investing in digital currencies a risky proposition, as investors can see their investments quickly lose value.

One of the reasons for the volatility of digital currencies is their relatively small market size compared to traditional currencies. While the total market capitalization of all digital currencies is in the hundreds of billions of dollars, this pales in comparison to the trillions of dollars traded in traditional currency markets every day.

This means that even small changes in demand for digital currencies can have a large impact on their value.

Another factor contributing to the volatility of digital currencies is the lack of regulation in the market. Unlike traditional financial markets, which are heavily regulated by governments and central banks, the digital currency market is largely unregulated. This lack of oversight can lead to market manipulation, fraud, and other illegal activities that can further increase the volatility of digital currencies.

In addition to volatility, digital currencies also face a number of other risks that investors should be aware of. One of the biggest risks is the threat of hacking and cyberattacks. Because digital currencies are stored electronically, they are vulnerable to hacking and theft. In fact, there have been several high-profile hacks of digital currency exchanges in recent years, resulting in millions of dollars worth of digital currencies being stolen.

Another risk facing digital currencies is regulatory uncertainty. While some countries have embraced digital currencies and are working to regulate them, others have banned or restricted their use. This regulatory uncertainty can create confusion and instability in the market, leading to increased volatility.

There is also the risk of technological obsolescence. While digital currencies like Bitcoin have been around for over a decade, the technology behind them is constantly evolving. New digital currencies are being created all the time, each with their own unique features and capabilities. This rapid pace of innovation can make it difficult for investors to keep up with the latest developments and assess the risks and rewards of investing in digital currencies.

Despite these risks, many investors are still drawn to digital currencies because of their potential for high returns. In recent years, there have been several success stories of investors who have made millions of dollars by investing in digital currencies. However, these success stories are the exception rather than the rule, and many investors have lost money by investing in digital currencies.

To mitigate the risks of investing in digital currencies, investors should take a number of precautions. One of the most important is to only invest money that they can afford to lose. Because of the high volatility of digital currencies, it is possible to lose a significant portion of your investment in a short period of time. By only investing money that you can afford to lose, you can protect yourself from financial ruin.

Investors should also do their due diligence before investing in digital currencies. This means researching the market, understanding the technology behind digital currencies, and staying informed about regulatory developments. By staying informed and educated, investors can make more informed decisions about their investments and reduce the risks of investing in digital currencies.

The volatility and risks of digital currencies make them a risky investment. While there is the potential for high returns, investors should be aware of the risks and take precautions to protect themselves.

By only investing money that they can afford to lose, doing their due diligence, and staying informed, investors can reduce the risks of investing in digital currencies and potentially profit from this exciting new asset class.

Chapter 4 :Analyzing Blockchain Data with Python

In this chapter, we will explore how to analyze blockchain data using Python. Blockchain technology has gained significant attention in recent years due to its decentralized and secure nature. By analyzing blockchain data, we can gain insights into transactions, network activity, and overall trends within the blockchain.

Python is a powerful programming language that is commonly used for data analysis and visualization tasks. By leveraging Python libraries such as Pandas, Matplotlib, and Seaborn, we can easily analyze blockchain data and extract valuable insights.

Understanding Blockchain Data

Before we dive into analyzing blockchain data, it's important to understand the structure of a blockchain. A blockchain is essentially a distributed ledger that stores a record of transactions in a secure and transparent manner. Each block in the blockchain contains a list of transactions, a timestamp, and a reference to the previous block, creating a chain of blocks.

Blockchain data is typically stored in a decentralized manner across multiple nodes in the network. This data can be accessed and analyzed using various tools and libraries, including Python.

Analyzing Blockchain Data with Python

To analyze blockchain data with Python, we first need to retrieve the data from the blockchain network. There are several ways to do this, including using APIs provided by blockchain platforms such as Bitcoin, Ethereum, or Ripple. Once we have obtained the data, we can process and analyze it using Python.

One common task when analyzing blockchain data is to calculate transaction volume and value over time. By aggregating and visualizing this data, we can gain insights into the overall activity and trends within the blockchain network.

We can also analyze network activity, such as the number of transactions, block size, and transaction fees. By monitoring these metrics, we can identify potential bottlenecks or issues within the blockchain network.

Another important aspect of analyzing blockchain data is to identify patterns and anomalies within the data. By applying statistical analysis and machine learning techniques, we can detect fraudulent activities, predict market trends, and optimize network performance.

Python Libraries for Blockchain Data Analysis

Python offers a wide range of libraries that are well-suited for analyzing blockchain data. Some of the most commonly used libraries include:

Pandas: Pandas is a powerful data manipulation library

that provides data structures and functions for analyzing structured data. It is commonly used for cleaning, transforming, and aggregating blockchain data.

Matplotlib: Matplotlib is a popular plotting library that allows us to create visualizations such as line charts, bar charts, and scatter plots. By visualizing blockchain data, we can gain a better understanding of trends and patterns within the data.

Seaborn: Seaborn is a statistical data visualization library that is built on top of Matplotlib. It provides additional plotting functions and themes for creating attractive and informative visualizations.

Scikit-learn: Scikit-learn is a machine learning library that provides tools for data mining, analysis, and modeling. By applying machine learning algorithms to blockchain data, we can uncover hidden patterns and make predictions based on historical data.

Analyzing blockchain data with Python can provide valuable insights into transactions, network activity, and overall trends within the blockchain. By leveraging Python libraries such as Pandas, Matplotlib, and Seaborn, we can easily process and visualize blockchain data to gain a better understanding of the underlying patterns and anomalies.

We will explore how to build predictive models using blockchain data and machine learning techniques. Stay tuned for more insights and practical examples of analyzing blockchain data with Python.

Introduction to Blockchain Technology

Blockchain technology is a revolutionary concept that has the potential to transform various industries and change the way we conduct transactions. In simple terms, a blockchain is a decentralized and distributed digital ledger that records transactions across a network of computers. Each transaction is recorded in a "block" that is linked to the previous block, forming a chain of blocks - hence the name "blockchain."

One of the key features of blockchain technology is its transparency and security. Because the ledger is distributed across a network of computers, it is extremely difficult for any one entity to control or manipulate the data. This makes blockchain technology highly secure and resistant to fraud and hacking.

Blockchain technology was first introduced in 2008 by an unknown person or group of people using the pseudonym Satoshi Nakamoto. It was originally created as the underlying technology for the digital currency Bitcoin, but its potential applications go far beyond just cryptocurrency.

One of the most promising applications of blockchain technology is in the financial industry. Banks and other financial institutions are exploring how blockchain technology can be used to streamline processes, reduce costs, and improve security. For example, blockchain technology could be used to facilitate cross-border payments, simplify the process of issuing and tracking loans, and improve the transparency of financial transactions.

Another industry that could benefit greatly from blockchain technology is supply chain management. By using blockchain technology to track the movement of goods from the manufacturer to the consumer, companies can improve transparency, reduce fraud, and ensure the authenticity of products. This could be particularly useful in industries such as food and pharmaceuticals, where traceability and authenticity are critical.

Blockchain technology also has the potential to revolutionize the healthcare industry. By securely storing patient records on a blockchain, healthcare providers can ensure the privacy and security of sensitive information, while also enabling patients to have more control over their own health data. This could lead to improved patient outcomes, reduced healthcare costs, and better collaboration among healthcare providers.

In addition to these industries, blockchain technology has the potential to impact a wide range of other sectors, including real estate, voting systems, intellectual property rights, and more. The possibilities are truly endless, and as the technology continues to evolve, we can expect to see even more innovative applications emerge.

Despite its potential, blockchain technology is still in its early stages, and there are many challenges that need to be addressed before it can be widely adopted. For example, scalability is a major issue, as current blockchain networks can only process a limited number of transactions per second. There are also concerns about energy consumption, as the process of "mining" new blocks requires a significant amount of computational power.

Despite these challenges, the future of blockchain technology looks bright. As more companies and industriesexplore the potential applications of blockchain technology, we can expect to see continued innovation and growth in this exciting field.

Whether it's improving transparency in supply chains, enhancing security in financial transactions, or revolutionizing healthcare records, blockchain technology has the potential to change the way we do business and interact with each other in the digital age.

Accessing and Analyzing Blockchain Data with python - scripts

Blockchain technology has revolutionized the way we think about data and transactions. With its decentralized and transparent nature, blockchain has the potential to disrupt various industries, including finance, supply chain, healthcare, and more. However, accessing and analyzing blockchain data can be a daunting task, especially for those who are new to the technology. In this article, we will explore how to access and analyze blockchain data using Python scripts.

Python is a popular programming language known for its simplicity and versatility. It is widely used in data analysis, machine learning, and web development. With the help of Python libraries such as web3.py, we can easily interact with blockchain networks and extract valuable data for analysis.

To get started with accessing blockchain data, we first need to connect to a blockchain network. In this example, we will use the Ethereum blockchain, one of the most popular and widely used blockchain networks. To connect to the Ethereum network, we need to install the web3.py library by running the following command:

```
pip install web3
```

Next, we need to create a Python script to connect to the

Ethereum network and retrieve blockchain data. Here is an example script that connects to the Ethereum network and retrieves the latest block number:

```python
from web3 import Web3

# Connect to the Ethereum network
w3                                           =
Web3(Web3.HTTPProvider('https://mainnet.infura.io/v3
/your_infura_project_id'))

# Get the latest block number latest_block =
w3.eth.blockNumber
print("Latest block number:", latest_block)
```

In this script, we import the Web3 class from the web3 library and create an instance of the Web3 class by providing the URL of an Ethereum node. In this example, we are using the Infura node, which is a popular service that provides access to Ethereum nodes. We then use the `eth.blockNumber` method to retrieve the latest block number on the Ethereum network.

Once we have connected to the blockchain network and retrieved some basic information, we can start analyzing blockchain data. One common task in blockchain analysis is to extract transaction data from a specific block.
Here is an example script that retrieves transaction data from a specific block on the Ethereum network:

```python
```

```
from web3 import Web3

# Connect to the Ethereum network

w3                                                    =
Web3(Web3.HTTPProvider('https://mainnet.infura.io/v3
/your_infura_project_id'))

# Get the block number block_number = 1234567

# Get the block hash
block_hash = w3.eth.get_block(block_number)['hash']

# Get the transactions in the block
transactions                                          =
w3.eth.get_block(block_hash)['transactions']

# Print the transaction datafor tx_hash in transactions:
tx = w3.eth.getTransaction(tx_hash) print("Transaction
hash:", tx.hash.hex())print("From:", tx['from'])
print("To:", tx['to'])
print("Value:", tx['value'])
print("Gas price:", tx['gasPrice'])
print("Gas used:", tx['gas'])
print("Block        number:",        tx['blockNumber'])
print("Timestamp:", tx['timestamp']) print()
```

In this script, we specify a block number and retrieve the
block hash using the `eth.get_block` method. We thenuse
the block hash to retrieve the transactions in the block and
print out the transaction data, including the transaction

hash, sender address, receiver address, value transferred, gas price, gas used, block number, and timestamp.

Another common task in blockchain analysis is to extract smart contract data from the blockchain. Smart contracts are self-executing contracts with the terms of the agreement between buyer and seller directly writteninto lines of code. Here is an example script that retrieves smart contract data from the Ethereum blockchain:

```python
from web3 import Web3

# Connect to the Ethereum network
w3 = Web3(Web3.HTTPProvider('https://mainnet.infura.io/v3/your_infura_project_id'))

# Specify the smart contract address contract_address = '0x123456789abcdef'

# Load the contract ABI
with open('contract_abi.json', 'r') as f: contract_abi = json.load(f)

# Create a contract instance
contract = w3.eth.contract(address=contract_address, abi=contract_abi)

# Get the contract name
contract_name = contract.functions.name().call()
print("Contract name:", contract_name)
```

```
# Get the total supply of tokens
total_supply        =        contract.functions.totalSupply().call()
print("Total supply:", total_supply)
```

In this script, we specify the address of a smart contract on the Ethereum blockchain and load the contract ABI (Application Binary Interface) from a JSON file. We then create a contract instance using the contract address and ABI, and use the `functions` attribute to call the `name` and `totalSupply`.

Chapter 5: Cryptocurrency Market Data Sources

In order to make informed decisions in the world of cryptocurrency trading, it is essential to have access to accurate and up-to-date market data. This data can help traders analyze trends, identify opportunities, and mitigate risks. In this chapter, we will explore the various sources of cryptocurrency market data and how they can be utilized effectively.

Cryptocurrency Exchanges

One of the primary sources of market data for cryptocurrencies is cryptocurrency exchanges. These platforms allow users to buy, sell, and trade various digital assets. Exchanges provide real-time data on prices, trading volumes, and market capitalization of different cryptocurrencies. Some popular cryptocurrency exchanges include Binance, Coinbase, and Kraken.

Traders can use exchange data to track the performance of specific cryptocurrencies, identify trading opportunities, and execute trades. It is important to note that each exchange may have slightly different pricing and volume data, so it is advisable to use multiple exchanges for a comprehensive view of the market.

CoinMarketCap

CoinMarketCap is a popular cryptocurrency data

aggregator that provides information on thousands of cryptocurrencies and tokens. The platform displays real-time prices, market capitalization, trading volumes, and historical data for each digital asset. CoinMarketCap also ranks cryptocurrencies based on various metrics such as market cap and trading volume.

Traders can use CoinMarketCap to monitor the overall performance of the cryptocurrency market, track specific coins or tokens, and compare different assets. The platform also provides news and analysis to help traders makeinformed decisions.

CoinGecko

CoinGecko is another cryptocurrency data aggregator that offers a wide range of market data and analysis tools.The platform provides information on prices, trading volumes, market capitalization, and historical data for thousands of cryptocurrencies. CoinGecko also ranks cryptocurrencies based on factors such as developer activity, community engagement, and liquidity.

Traders can use CoinGecko to track the performance of specific cryptocurrencies, identify emerging trends, and discover new investment opportunities. The platform also offers portfolio tracking and price alerts to help traders stay informed.

Cryptocurrency News Websites

Cryptocurrency news websites such as CoinDesk, Cointelegraph, and CryptoSlate are valuable sources of market data and analysis. These platforms provide news, insights, and updates on the latest developments in the cryptocurrency industry. Traders can use news websites to stay informed about market trends, regulatory changes, and technological advancements.

In addition to news articles, cryptocurrency news websites often publish market analysis, price predictions, and interviews with industry experts. Traders can leverage this information to make informed decisions and stay ahead of the curve.

Social Media and Forums

Social media platforms such as Twitter, Reddit, and Telegram are popular channels for cryptocurrency enthusiasts to discuss market trends and share insights. Traders can follow influential figures in the cryptocurrency space, join relevant groups and communities, and participate in discussions to stay informed about the latest developments.

Cryptocurrency forums such as Bitcointalk and CryptoCompare also provide a platform for traders to exchange ideas, ask questions, and share information. These forums can be valuable sources of market data, analysis, and tips for traders looking to navigate the complex world of cryptocurrency trading.

There are various sources of cryptocurrency market data that traders can leverage to make informed decisions. By utilizing exchanges, data aggregators, news websites, social media, and forums, traders can stay informed about market trends, identify opportunities, and mitigate risks. It is important to conduct thorough research and due diligence before making any investment decisions in the volatile world of cryptocurrencies.

Popular Cryptocurrency Exchanges

Cryptocurrency exchanges have become an integral part of the digital currency ecosystem. These platforms allow users to buy, sell, and trade various cryptocurrencies, making it easier for investors to access the volatile and fast-paced world of digital assets. With the rise in popularity of cryptocurrencies like Bitcoin, Ethereum, and Litecoin, there has been a corresponding increase in the number of cryptocurrency exchanges available to users.

In this article, we will take a closer look at some of the most popular cryptocurrency exchanges in the market today. These exchanges have gained a reputation for their reliability, security, and user-friendly interfaces, making them go-to choices for both novice and experienced cryptocurrency traders.

Binance

Binance is one of the largest and most popular cryptocurrency exchanges in the world. Launched in 2017, Binance quickly rose to prominence thanks to its wide range of supported cryptocurrencies, low trading fees, and robust security measures. The platform offers a user-friendly interface that caters to both beginners and advanced traders, making it a top choice for many cryptocurrency enthusiasts.

One of the key features of Binance is its extensive range of trading pairs, which allows users to trade a wide variety of cryptocurrencies against major fiat currencies like USD,

EUR, and GBP. The exchange also offers advanced trading options like margin trading and futures contracts, giving experienced traders the tools they need to maximize their profits.

In terms of security, Binance has a strong track record of protecting user funds and data from cyber threats. The exchange uses industry-leading security measures like two-factor authentication and cold storage to keep user assets safe from hackers.

Overall, Binance is a top choice for cryptocurrency traders looking for a reliable and feature-rich exchange with a strong reputation in the industry.

Coinbase

Coinbase is another popular cryptocurrency exchange that has gained a loyal following thanks to its user-friendly interface and strong security measures. Launched in 2012, Coinbase is one of the oldest and most trusted exchanges in the market, making it a go-to choice for many new cryptocurrency investors.

One of the key features of Coinbase is its ease of use, which makes it a great option for beginners looking to get started with cryptocurrency trading. The platform offers a simple and intuitive interface that allows users to buy, sell, and store cryptocurrencies with ease. Coinbase also offers a mobile app that makes it easy to trade on the go, further enhancing its accessibility.

In terms of security, Coinbase has a strong track record of

protecting user funds and data from cyber threats. The exchange uses industry-leading security measures like two-factor authentication and cold storage to keep user assets safe from hackers.

Overall, Coinbase is a top choice for cryptocurrency traders looking for a reliable and user-friendly exchange with a strong reputation in the industry.

Kraken

Kraken is a well-established cryptocurrency exchange that has gained a reputation for its robust security measures and wide range of supported cryptocurrencies. Launched in 2011, Kraken is one of the oldest exchanges in the market, making it a trusted choice for many experienced cryptocurrency traders.

One of the key features of Kraken is its strong focus on security, with the exchange implementing industry-leading security measures like two-factor authentication and cold storage to protect user funds and data. Kraken also has a strong track record of responding quickly to security incidents, further enhancing its reputation as a secure exchange.

In terms of supported cryptocurrencies, Kraken offers a wide range of trading pairs, allowing users to trade popular cryptocurrencies like Bitcoin, Ethereum, and Litecoin against major fiat currencies like USD, EUR, and GBP. The exchange also offers advanced trading options like margin trading and futures contracts, giving experienced traders the tools they need to maximize their profits.

Overall, Kraken is a top choice for cryptocurrency traders looking for a secure and reliable exchange with a wide range of supported cryptocurrencies.

Bitfinex

Bitfinex is a popular cryptocurrency exchange known for its advanced trading features and high liquidity. Launched in 2012, Bitfinex quickly gained a reputation as a go-to platform for experienced cryptocurrency traders looking for a wide range of trading options.

One of the key features of Bitfinex is its advanced trading platform, which offers a wide range of trading tools and options for users. The exchange supports margin trading, lending, and futures contracts, allowing traders to maximize their profits and manage their risk effectively. Bitfinex also offers a wide range of trading pairs, allowing users to trade popular cryptocurrencies like Bitcoin, Ethereum, and Ripple against major fiat currencies like USD, EUR, and JPY.

Accessing Market Data via APIs with python - scripts

Accessing market data has become easier than ever before thanks to the use of Application Programming Interfaces (APIs). APIs allow developers to access and interact with data from various sources, including financial markets, in a streamlined and efficient manner. In this article, we will explore how to access market data via APIs using Python scripts as examples.

Python is a popular programming language known for its simplicity and versatility, making it an ideal choice for working with APIs. By leveraging Python's powerful libraries such as requests and pandas, developers can easily retrieve and manipulate market data to make informed decisions.

To begin accessing market data via APIs with Python, the first step is to identify the API that provides the data you are interested in. Many financial institutions and data providers offer APIs that allow developers to access real-time and historical market data. Some popular APIs include Alpha Vantage, Yahoo Finance, and Quandl.

Once you have chosen an API to work with, the next step is to obtain an API key. An API key is a unique identifier that grants you access to the API's data. You can usually obtain an API key by signing up for an account on the API provider's website and following their instructions for authentication.

With your API key in hand, you can now begin writing Python scripts to access market data. Let's walk through an example using the Alpha Vantage API, which provides free access to real-time and historical stock market data.

First, you will need to install the requests library, which allows you to make HTTP requests in Python. You can install the requests library using pip by running the following command in your terminal:

```
```

```
pip install requests
```
```

Next, you can create a Python script to access market data from the Alpha Vantage API. Here is an example script that retrieves the latest stock price for a given symbol:

```python
import requests

API_KEY = 'YOUR_API_KEY'
symbol = 'AAPL'

url = f'https://www.alphavantage.co/query?function=GLOBAL_QUOTE&symbol={symbol}&apikey={API_KEY}'

response = requests.get(url)
data = response.json()

latest_price = data['Global Quote']['05. price']

print(f'The latest price of {symbol} is ${latest_price}')
```
```

```
```

In this script, we first define our API key and the stock symbol we are interested in (in this case, Apple Inc. with the symbol AAPL). We then construct the API URL using the symbol and API key, and make a GET request to retrieve the data.

The response from the API is in JSON format, which we can parse using the json() method provided by the requests library. We extract the latest price from the response data and print it to the console.

This is just a simple example of how you can access market data using Python scripts. Depending on the API you are working with, you may need to adjust the URL and data parsing logic accordingly. It is important to read the API documentation provided by the API provider to understand how to structure your requests and handle the response data.

In addition to retrieving real-time stock prices, you can also use Python scripts to access historical market data for backtesting and analysis. For example, you can retrieve historical stock prices for a given symbol and date range using the Alpha Vantage API's TIME_SERIES_DAILY endpoint:

```python
import requests
import pandas as pd

API_KEY = 'YOUR_API_KEY'
symbol = 'AAPL' start_date = '2022-01-01'
```

```
end_date = '2022-01-31'

url                                                    =
f'https://www.alphavantage.co/query?function=TIME_SERI
ES_DAILY&symbol={symbol}&apikey={AP I_KEY}'

response = requests.get(url)data = response.json()

df = pd.DataFrame(data['Time Series (Daily)']).Tdf.index
= pd.to_datetime(df.index)
df  =  df[(df.index  >=  start_date)  &  (df.index  <=
end_date)]

print(df)
```

In this script, we retrieve daily stock price data for Apple Inc. for the month of January 2022. We parse the response data into a pandas DataFrame for easy manipulation and analysis. By using Python scripts like this, you can access and analyze historical market data to gain insights into stock performance over time.

In conclusion, accessing market data via APIs with Python is a powerful tool for developers and traders alike. By leveraging Python's libraries and scripting capabilities, you can easily retrieve, manipulate, and analyze market data to inform your investment decisions. Whether you are interested in real-time stock prices, historical data, or other financial metrics, Python scripts can help you access the information you need in a fast and efficient manner. Experiment with different APIs and data sources to explore the vast world of market data and unlock new opportunities for success.

Chapter 6: Technical Analysis for Cryptocurrency Trading

Technical analysis is a crucial tool for traders looking to make informed decisions in the volatile world of cryptocurrency trading. By analyzing historical price data and market trends, traders can gain valuable insights into potential future price movements and make more strategic trading decisions.

In this chapter, we will explore the basics of technical analysis and how it can be applied to cryptocurrency trading. We will cover key technical indicators, chart patterns, and other tools that can help traders identify potential entry and exit points in the market. By understanding the principles of technical analysis, traders can improve their trading strategies and increase their chances of success in the cryptocurrency market.

Understanding Technical Analysis

Technical analysis is a method of analyzing financial markets that relies on historical price data and market trends to predict future price movements. Unlike fundamental analysis, which focuses on the underlying value of an asset, technical analysis is based solely on price action and market psychology.

There are many different tools and techniques that traders can use to conduct technical analysis, but the most common include chart patterns, technical indicators, and support and resistance levels. By studying these factors, traders can gain valuable insights into market trends and make more informed trading decisions.

One of the key principles of technical analysis is that price movements are not random, but rather follow certain patterns and trends that can be identified and analyzed. By studying these patterns, traders can gain a better understanding of market dynamics and make more accurate predictions about future price movements.

Key Technical Indicators

Technical indicators are mathematical calculations based on price and volume data that can help traders identify potential entry and exit points in the market. There are many different technical indicators available, but some of the most commonly used in cryptocurrency trading include:

Moving Averages: Moving averages are one of the simplest and most widely used technical indicators. They calculate the average price of an asset over a specific period of time and are used to identify trends and potential support and resistance levels.

Relative Strength Index (RSI): The RSI is a momentum oscillator that measures the speed and change of price movements. It ranges from 0 to 100 and is used to identify overbought and oversold conditions in the market.

Bollinger Bands: Bollinger Bands are volatility bands that are placed above and below a moving average. They are used to identify potential price breakouts and reversals in the market.

MACD (Moving Average Convergence Divergence): The MACD is a trend-following momentum indicator that shows the relationship between two moving averages of an asset's price. It is used to identify changes in the strength and direction of a trend.

Chart Patterns

Chart patterns are another important tool in the technical analyst's toolkit. These patterns are formed by price movements on a chart and can help traders identify potential entry and exit points in the market. Some of the most common chart patterns include:

Head and Shoulders: The head and shoulders pattern is a reversal pattern that indicates a potential trend reversal. It consists of three peaks, with the middle peak (the head) being higher than the other two (the shoulders).

Double Top/Bottom: The double top/bottom pattern is a reversal pattern that indicates a potential trend reversal. It consists of two peaks or troughs that are roughly equal in height, with a valley or peak in between.

Triangle Patterns: Triangle patterns are continuation patterns that indicate a period of consolidation before a potential breakout. There are several types of triangle patterns, including ascending, descending, and symmetrical triangles.

Support and Resistance Levels

Support and resistance levels are key concepts in technical analysis that can help traders identify potential price levels where a trend may reverse or accelerate. Support levels are price levels where a downtrend is likely to reverse, while resistance levels are price levels where an uptrend is likely to reverse.

By identifying these key levels on a chart, traders can set stop-loss orders, take-profit targets, and other risk management strategies to protect their capital and maximize their profits. Support and resistance levels can also help traders identify potential entry and exit points in the market.

Technical analysis is a powerful tool for traders looking to navigate the complex and volatile world of cryptocurrency trading. By studying historical price data, market trends, and key technical indicators, traders can gain valuable insights into potential price movements and make more informed trading decisions.

In this chapter, we covered the basics of technical analysis and how it can be applied to cryptocurrency trading. We discussed key technical indicators, chart patterns, and support and resistance levels that can help traders identify potential entry and exit points in the market.

By understanding these principles and incorporating them into their trading strategies, traders can improve their chances of success in the cryptocurrency market. Whether you are a beginner or an experienced trader, mastering the principles of technical analysis can help you become a more successful and profitable trader in the fast-paced world of cryptocurrency trading.

Technical Analysis in Cryptocurrency Trading

Technical analysis is a popular method used by traders to predict future price movements in the cryptocurrency market. It involves analyzing historical price data, volume, and other market indicators to identify patterns and trends that can help traders make informed decisions about when to buy or sell cryptocurrencies.

One of the key principles of technical analysis is that historical price movements tend to repeat themselves, and that past performance can be a good indicator of future performance. By studying charts and graphs of price data, traders can identify patterns such as support and resistance levels, trend lines, and chart patterns that can help them predict where prices are likely to go next.

Support and resistance levels are key concepts in technical analysis. Support levels are price levels at which a cryptocurrency has historically had difficulty falling below, while resistance levels are price levels at which a cryptocurrency has historically had difficulty rising above. When a cryptocurrency breaks through a support or resistance level, it can signal a trend reversal or continuation, depending on the direction of the breakout.

Trend lines are another important tool in technical analysis. Trend lines are lines drawn on a chart that connect the highs or lows of a cryptocurrency's price movements over a certain period of time. An uptrend line connects the lows of a cryptocurrency's price movements, while a downtrend line connects the highs. When a cryptocurrency's price breaks through a trend line, it can signal a change in the direction of the trend.

Chart patterns are also commonly used in technical analysis. Chart patterns are formations that appear on a price chart that can help traders predict future price movements. Some common chart patterns include head and shoulders patterns, double tops and bottoms, and triangles. By recognizing these patterns, traders can make more informed decisions about when to enter or exit a trade.

In addition to these technical indicators, traders also use technical analysis tools such as moving averages, MACD (Moving Average Convergence Divergence), RSI (Relative Strength Index), and Bollinger Bands to helpthem make trading decisions. Moving averages are used to smooth out price data and identify trends, while MACD is used to identify changes in momentum. RSI is a momentum oscillator that measures the speed and change of price movements, while Bollinger Bands are used to identify overbought or oversold conditions.

While technical analysis can be a useful tool for predicting future price movements in the cryptocurrency market, it is important to remember that it is not foolproof. Market conditions can change rapidly, and unexpected events can cause prices to move in ways that are not predicted by technical analysis. Traders should also be aware of the limitations of technical analysis, such as the fact that it is based on historical data and cannotpredict future events.

Despite these limitations, many traders find technical

analysis to be a valuable tool in their trading arsenal. By using technical analysis to identify patterns and trends in the market, traders can make more informed decisions about when to buy or sell cryptocurrencies. Technical analysis can also help traders set stop-loss orders and take-profit targets to manage their risk and maximize their profits.

technical analysis is a valuable tool for traders in the cryptocurrency market. By studying historical price data, volume, and other market indicators, traders can identify patterns and trends that can help them predict future price movements. While technical analysis is not foolproof, it can be a useful tool for making informed trading decisions and managing risk.

Traders should be aware of the limitations of technical analysis and use it in conjunction with other tools and strategies to maximize their chances of success in the cryptocurrency market.

Implementing Technical Indicators in Python with python - scripts

Technical indicators are essential tools used by traders and analysts to make informed decisions when trading in financial markets. These indicators are mathematical calculations based on historical price, volume, or open interest data. They help traders identify trends, momentum, volatility, and potential reversal points in the market.

In this article, we will discuss how to implement technical indicators in Python using the popular library called `ta` (Technical Analysis Library). The `ta` library provides a wide range of technical indicators that can be easily integrated into your trading strategies.

To get started, you need to install the `ta` library using the following command:

```
pip install ta
```

Once the library is installed, you can start using it to calculate various technical indicators. Let's take a look at an example of how to calculate the Moving Average Convergence Divergence (MACD) indicator using the `ta` library:

```python
import pandas as pd
```

```
from ta.trend import MACD

# Load historical price data
data = pd.read_csv('historical_data.csv')

# Calculate MACD indicator macd = MACD(data['Close'])

# Add MACD values to the dataframe data['macd'] =
macd.macd()    data['macd_signal']    =    macd.macd_signal()
data['macd_diff'] = macd.macd_diff()

print(data)
```

In this example, we first load historical price data from a CSV file using the `pd.read_csv()` function. We then calculate the MACD indicator using the `MACD` class from the `ta.trend` module. Finally, we add the MACD values to the dataframe and print the updated dataframe.

The `ta` library provides a wide range of technical indicators, including moving averages, Relative Strength Index (RSI), Bollinger Bands, and many more. You can explore the full list of available indicators in the library documentation.

In addition to using the `ta` library, you can also implement custom technical indicators in Python using the `pandas` library and NumPy. Let's take a look at an example of how to calculate the Simple Moving Average (SMA) indicator using these libraries:

```python
import pandas as pdimport numpy as np

# Load historical price data
data = pd.read_csv('historical_data.csv')

# Calculate SMA indicator
data['sma'] = data['Close'].rolling(window=20).mean()

print(data)
```

In this example, we use the `rolling()` function from the `pandas` library to calculate the SMA indicator with a window of 20 periods. We then add the SMA values to the dataframe and print the updated dataframe.

Implementing technical indicators in Python allows you to analyze historical price data and make informed trading decisions based on market trends. By using libraries like `ta` and `pandas`, you can easily calculate a widerange of technical indicators and integrate them into your trading strategies.

In addition to calculating technical indicators, you can also visualize them using libraries like `matplotlib` and `seaborn`. Visualizing technical indicators can help you better understand market trends and make moreinformed trading decisions.

78

Let's take a look at an example of how to visualize the SMA indicator using the `matplotlib` library:

```python
import matplotlib.pyplot as plt

# Plot historical price data plt.figure(figsize=(12, 6))
plt.plot(data['Close'], label='Close Price')

# Plot SMA indicator
plt.plot(data['sma'], label='SMA', color='red')

plt.title('Simple Moving Average (SMA)')plt.xlabel('Date')
plt.ylabel('Price')plt.legend() plt.show()
```

In this example, we use the `plot()` function from the `matplotlib` library to plot the historical price data and the

SMA indicator on the same chart. We then customize the plot with labels, titles, and legends before displaying it using the `show()` function.

Visualizing technical indicators can provide valuable insights into market trends and help you identify potential trading opportunities. By combining technical analysis with visualization techniques, you can improve your trading strategies and make more informed decisions.

In conclusion, implementing technical indicators in Python is a powerful tool for traders and analysts looking to analyze market trends and make informed trading decisions. By using libraries like `ta` and `pandas`, you can easily calculate a wide range of technical indicators and integrate them into your trading strategies.

In addition to calculating technical indicators, you can also visualize them using libraries like `matplotlib` and `seaborn`. Visualizing technical indicators can help you better understand market trends and identify potential trading opportunities.

Whether you are a beginner or an experienced trader, learning how to implement technical indicators in Python can help you improve your trading strategies and make more informed decisions in the financial markets. So, start exploring the world of technical analysis in Python and take your trading to the next level!

Chapter 7: Developing Trading Bots with Python

In today's fast-paced financial markets, having the ability to automate trading strategies can give traders a significant edge. Trading bots, also known as algorithmic trading systems, are computer programs that execute trades based on predefined criteria. In this chapter, we will explore how to develop trading bots using Python, a powerful and versatile programming language.

Python is a popular choice for developing trading bots due to its simplicity, readability, and extensive library support. With Python, traders can easily access market data, perform technical analysis, and execute trades across multiple exchanges. In this chapter, we will cover the basics of developing trading bots with Python, including setting up a development environment, accessing market data, implementing trading strategies, and executing trades.

Setting up a Development Environment

Before we can start developing trading bots with Python, we need to set up a development environment. This involves installing the necessary libraries and tools, such as Python, a code editor, and any additional libraries for accessing market data and executing trades. One popular choice for developing trading bots is the Jupyter Notebook, a web-based interactive computing environment that allows for easy code execution and visualization.

To set up a development environment for developing trading bots with Python, follow these steps:

Install Python: Python can be downloaded from the official website (https://www.python.org/) and installed on your computer.

Install a code editor: Choose a code editor that supports Python, such as Visual Studio Code, PyCharm, or Jupyter Notebook.

Install necessary libraries: Install libraries such as pandas, numpy, matplotlib, and ccxt for accessing market data and executing trades.

Set up API keys: To access market data and execute trades, you will need to set up API keys with the exchanges you plan to trade on.

Accessing Market Data

Once we have set up our development environment, we can start accessing market data using Python. Market data is essential for developing trading strategies, as it provides insights into price movements, volume, and other key indicators. Python libraries such as ccxt and pandas can be used to access market data from various exchanges and perform technical analysis.

To access market data using Python, follow these steps:

Initialize the ccxt library: Import the ccxt library and create an instance of the exchange you want to access data from.

Fetch market data: Use the ccxt library to fetch historical market data for a specific trading pair, such as Bitcoin/USD or Ethereum/USD.

Perform technical analysis: Use libraries such as pandas and numpy to perform technical analysis on the market data, such as calculating moving averages, RSI, and MACD.

Implementing Trading Strategies

With access to market data, we can now implement trading strategies using Python. Trading strategies are rules or algorithms that determine when to buy or sell assets based on market conditions. Python provides a flexible and powerful framework for implementing trading strategies, allowing traders to backtest and optimize their strategies before deploying them in live markets.

To implement trading strategies using Python, follow these steps:

Define trading signals: Define trading signals based on technical indicators, such as moving averages, RSI, and MACD.

Implement buy and sell logic: Implement buy and sell logic based on the trading signals generated by the technical indicators.

Backtest the strategy: Backtest the trading strategy using historical market data to evaluate its performance and profitability.

Executing Trades

Once we have implemented and backtested our trading strategy, we can now execute trades using Python.Python libraries such as ccxt and requests can be used to interact with exchange APIs and execute trades automatically based on predefined criteria. By automating the trading process, traders can capitalize on opportunities in the market without the need for manual intervention.

To execute trades using Python, follow these steps:

Initialize the exchange API: Import the ccxt library and create an instance of the exchange you want to tradeon.

Place buy and sell orders: Use the exchange API to place buy and sell orders based on the trading signalsgenerated by your strategy.

Monitor trade execution: Monitor the execution of trades and adjust the strategy as needed to optimizeperformance.

Python's simplicity, readability, and extensive library support make it an ideal choice for developing trading bots, allowing traders to capitalize on opportunities in the market with ease. By mastering the art of developing trading bots with Python, traders can take their trading to the next level and achieve their financial goals.

Introduction to Trading Bots

Trading bots have become an increasingly popular tool for traders in the financial markets. These automated programs are designed to execute trades on behalf of the user, based on a set of predefined criteria. In this article, we will provide an introduction to trading bots, how they work, and the benefits and risks associated with using them.

What are trading bots?

Trading bots are software programs that interact with financial exchanges to automatically execute trades on behalf of the user. These bots can be programmed to follow a specific trading strategy, such as buying or selling a particular asset when certain conditions are met. Some trading bots are designed to be used with specific exchanges, while others can be used across multiple platforms.

How do trading bots work?

Trading bots work by analyzing market data and executing trades based on predefined rules. These rules can be as simple as buying or selling a particular asset at a certain price, or more complex strategies that involve multiple indicators and signals. The bot will continuously monitor market conditions and execute trades when the criteria are met.

There are two main types of trading bots: rule-based bots

and AI-based bots. Rule-based bots follow a set of predefined rules, while AI-based bots use machine learning algorithms to adapt to changing market conditions. Both types of bots have their own advantages and disadvantages, depending on the trading strategy and the level of risk the user is willing to take.

Benefits of using trading bots

There are several benefits to using trading bots. One of the main advantages is that they can execute trades much faster than a human trader, which can be crucial in fast-moving markets. Bots can also operate 24/7, allowing traders to take advantage of opportunities that may arise outside of regular trading hours.

Another benefit of trading bots is that they can eliminate emotions from trading decisions. Emotions such as fear and greed can cloud judgment and lead to poor trading decisions. Bots operate based on predefined rules and do not have emotions, which can help traders stick to their strategy and avoid making impulsive decisions.

Additionally, trading bots can backtest trading strategies using historical data to see how they would have performed in the past. This can help traders optimize their strategies and identify potential weaknesses before risking real money.

Risks of using trading bots

While trading bots offer several benefits, there are also risks associated with using them. One of the main risks is that bots can malfunction or be hacked, leading to unexpected losses. It is important for traders to thoroughly test their bots and ensure they have proper security measures in place to protect their accounts.

Another risk is that bots can be susceptible to market manipulation. In some cases, traders may use bots to artificially inflate or deflate the price of an asset, leading to losses for other traders. It is important for traders to be aware of these risks and take steps to mitigate them.

Additionally, trading bots can be complex to set up and require a certain level of technical knowledge. Traders may need to spend time learning how to program their bots and optimize their strategies, which can be time-consuming.

Trading bots are a powerful tool for traders in the financial markets, offering the ability to execute trades quickly and efficiently. While there are risks associated with using bots, the benefits can outweigh the drawbacks for many traders.

It is important for traders to thoroughly test their bots and understand the risks involved before using them in live trading. With proper risk management and security measures in place, trading bots can be a valuable asset for traders looking to automate their trading strategies.

Building Your First Trading Bot with python - scripts

Trading bots have become increasingly popular in the world of finance, allowing traders to automate their trading strategies and execute trades without human intervention. These bots can be programmed to analyze market data, make trading decisions, and execute trades based on predefined criteria. In this article, we will explore how to build your first trading bot using Python.

Python is a popular programming language for building trading bots due to its simplicity and versatility. It has a wide range of libraries and tools that make it easy to work with financial data and execute trades. In this tutorial, we will use the ccxt library, which provides a simple and consistent API for interacting with various cryptocurrency exchanges.

To get started, you will need to install the ccxt library by running the following command:

```
pip install ccxt
```

Once you have installed the ccxt library, you can start building your trading bot. In this example, we will create a simple bot that buys and sells Bitcoin based on the current price. Here is the code for our trading bot:

```python
import ccxt
```

```python
# Create an instance of the Binance exchange binance = ccxt.binance()

# Get the current price of Bitcoin symbol = 'BTC/USDT'
ticker = binance.fetch_ticker(symbol)price = ticker['last']

# Define the buy and sell prices buy_price = price * 0.95
sell_price = price * 1.05

# Check the current balance of USDT
usdt_balance = binance.fetch_balance()['USDT']['free']

# Check if the current price is below the buy price if price < buy_price and usdt_balance > 0:
amount = usdt_balance / price
order = binance.create_market_buy_order(symbol, amount) print('Bought {} Bitcoin at {}'.format(amount, price))

# Check if the current price is above the sell price
```

```
elif price > sell_price:
amount = binance.fetch_balance()['BTC']['free']
order    =    binance.create_market_sell_order(symbol,
amount) print('Sold {} Bitcoin at {}'.format(amount,
price))
```

In this code snippet, we first create an instance of the
Binance exchange using the ccxt library. We then fetch the
current price of Bitcoin in USDT and define the buy and
sell prices as 5% below and above the current price,
respectively. We also check the current balance of USDT
in our account.

Next, we check if the current price is below the buy price
and if we have enough USDT balance to buy Bitcoin. If
both conditions are met, we calculate the amount of
Bitcoin we can buy with our available USDT balance and
execute a market buy order. Similarly, if the current price
is above the sell price, we sell all our Bitcoin holdings using
a market sell order.

This is a very basic example of a trading bot, and there are
many ways to improve and expand upon it. For instance,
you could add more sophisticated trading strategies, risk
management techniques, and technical indicators to make
your bot more profitable and resilient in different market
conditions.

It is important to note that building and running a trading
bot involves risks, and you should always use caution and
do your own research before deploying a bot in live
trading. Make sure to test your bot thoroughly in a

simulated environment before trading with real money.

In addition to the ccxt library, there are many other libraries and tools available for building trading bots in Python. Some popular ones include backtrader, zipline, and quantconnect. These libraries provide a wide range of features for backtesting, optimizing, and deploying trading strategies in various financial markets.

Overall, building a trading bot with Python can be a rewarding and educational experience for traders looking to automate their strategies and improve their trading performance. By leveraging the power of Python and its rich ecosystem of libraries, you can create a bot that is capable of executing complex trading strategies and adapting to changing market conditions.

In conclusion, building your first trading bot with Python is a great way to learn about algorithmic trading and explore the exciting world of automated trading. With the right tools and knowledge, you can create a bot that is capable of executing profitable trades and generating consistent returns. So why not give it a try and start building your own trading bot today?

Chapter 8: Backtesting Trading Strategies

Backtesting trading strategies is an essential step in the development and validation of any trading strategy. It involves testing a trading strategy on historical data to evaluate its performance and profitability. By backtesting a strategy, traders can gain valuable insights into how it would have performed in the past and identify any potential weaknesses or areas for improvement.

The first step in backtesting a trading strategy is to define the rules and parameters of the strategy. This includes determining the entry and exit points, stop-loss levels, profit targets, and any other criteria that will be used to make trading decisions. Once the rules are defined, the next step is to apply them to historical market data to see how the strategy would have performed in real market conditions.

There are several tools and platforms available for backtesting trading strategies, ranging from simple spreadsheet programs to more advanced software specifically designed for this purpose. Some popular backtesting platforms include MetaTrader, NinjaTrader, and TradeStation, which allow traders to test their strategies on historical data and analyze the results.

When backtesting a trading strategy, it is important to use a large and representative sample of historical data to ensure the results are reliable and accurate. Traders should also take into account factors such as slippage, commissions, and trading costs when backtesting a strategy, as these can have a significant impact on its performance.

One of the key benefits of backtesting trading strategies is that it allows traders to evaluate the performance of a strategy without risking real money. By testing a strategy on historical data, traders can gain confidence in its effectiveness and make any necessary adjustments before implementing it in live trading.

In addition to evaluating the performance of a trading strategy, backtesting can also be used to optimize and refine the strategy. By analyzing the results of the backtest, traders can identify patterns and trends in the data that can help them improve the strategy and make it more profitable.

It is important to note that backtesting trading strategies is not a foolproof method of predicting future performance. Market conditions can change, and what worked well in the past may not necessarily work in the future. However, by backtesting a strategy on a large sample of historical data, traders can gain valuable insights into its potential performance and make more informed decisions when trading live.

Backtesting trading strategies is an essential step in the development and validation of any trading strategy. By testing a strategy on historical data, traders can evaluate its performance, identify weaknesses, and make any necessary adjustments before implementing it in live trading.

While backtesting is not a guarantee of future success, it can provide valuable insights that can help traders improve their trading strategies and make more informed decisions in the market.

Importance of Backtesting Trading Strategies

Backtesting trading strategies is a crucial step in the process of developing a successful trading system. It involves testing a trading strategy using historical data to see how it would have performed in the past. By backtesting a trading strategy, traders can evaluate its potential profitability and risk before risking real money in the markets. In this article, we will discuss the importance of backtesting trading strategies and why it is essential for traders to incorporate this step into their trading process.

One of the primary reasons why backtesting trading strategies is important is that it allows traders to evaluate the performance of their trading system in a controlled environment. By using historical data, traders can see how their strategy would have performed in various market conditions and scenarios. This can help traders identify any weaknesses or flaws in their strategy and make necessary adjustments before putting real money on the line.

Another key benefit of backtesting trading strategies is that it can help traders gain confidence in their system. By seeing how their strategy has performed in the past, traders can have more faith in their system's ability to generate profits. This confidence can help traders stick to their trading plan during periods of drawdowns or losses, which is essential for long-term success in trading.

Additionally, backtesting trading strategies can help traders optimize their trading system for better performance. By analyzing the results of their backtests, traders can identify areas where their strategy can be improved or optimized. This could involve tweaking parameters, adding new rules, or removing ineffective elements from the strategy. By continuously backtesting and optimizing their trading system, traders can increase their chances of success in the markets.

Furthermore, backtesting trading strategies can help traders understand the risks associated with their system. By analyzing the historical performance of their strategy, traders can get a better sense of the potential drawdowns and losses they may experience in the future. This can help traders set realistic expectations and manage their risk accordingly. Understanding the risks associated with a trading strategy is crucial for protecting capital and avoiding large losses in the markets.

In addition to evaluating performance and managing risk, backtesting trading strategies can also help traders gain valuable insights into market behavior. By analyzing historical data, traders can see how their strategy performs in different market conditions, such as trending markets, ranging markets, or high volatility periods. This can help traders understand how their system reacts to various market environments and make informed decisions about when to trade and when to stay on the sidelines.

Overall, backtesting trading strategies is an essential step in the process of developing a successful trading system. It allows traders to evaluate performance, gain confidence, optimize their system, manage risk, and gain valuable insights into market behavior. By incorporating backtesting into their trading process, traders can increase their chances of success in the markets and achieve their trading goals.

In conclusion, backtesting trading strategies is a critical step in the process of developing a successful trading system. By testing a trading strategy using historical data, traders can evaluate performance, gain confidence, optimize their system, manage risk, and gain valuable insights into market behavior. Incorporating backtesting into the trading process can help traders increase their chances of success in the markets and achieve their trading goals.

Implementing Backtesting in Python - scripts

Backtesting is a crucial step in the development and evaluation of trading strategies. It involves testing a strategy against historical data to determine its effectiveness and potential profitability. By implementing backtesting in Python, traders can automate this process and gain valuable insights into their strategies' performance.

In this article, we will discuss how to implement backtesting in Python using scripts and provide examples to demonstrate the process.

Getting Started with Backtesting in Python

To get started with backtesting in Python, you will need to install the necessary libraries. The most commonly used library for backtesting in Python is `Backtrader`. You can install it using pip by running the following command:

```bash
pip install backtrader
```

Once you have installed the library, you can start coding your backtesting scripts. Creating a Simple Backtesting Script
Let's start by creating a simple backtesting script that buys and sells a stock based on a moving average crossover strategy. In this strategy, we will buy when the short-term moving average crosses above the long-term moving

average and sell when the short-term moving average crosses below the long-term moving average.

Here is the code for the backtesting script:

```python
import backtrader as bt

class MovingAverageCrossStrategy(bt.Strategy):
params = ( ('sma1', 50),
('sma2', 200),
)

def __init__(self):
self.sma1 = bt.indicators.SimpleMovingAverage(self.data.close, period=self.params.sma1)                self.sma2 = bt.indicators.SimpleMovingAverage(self.data.close, period=self.params.sma2)

def next(self):
if self.sma1 > self.sma2:self.buy()
elif self.sma1 < self.sma2:self.sell()
```

```
cerebro                      =              bt.Cerebro()
cerebro.addstrategy(MovingAverageCrossStrategy)

data  =  bt.feeds.YahooFinanceData(dataname='AAPL',
fromdate=datetime(2010, 1, 1), todate=datetime(2020, 1,
1))
cerebro.adddata(data)

cerebro.run()cerebro.plot()
```

In this script, we define a `MovingAverageCrossStrategy` class that inherits from `bt.Strategy`. We define two parameters `sma1` and `sma2` for the short-term and long-term moving averages, respectively. In the `_____init _____`method, we calculate the moving averages using the `bt.indicators.SimpleMovingAverage` function.

In the `next` method, we implement the trading logic. If the short-term moving average is greater than the long-term moving average, we buy the stock. If the short-term moving average is less than the long-term moving average, we sell the stock.

We then create a `Cerebro` instance, add the `MovingAverageCrossStrategy` to it, and add historical data for the stock `AAPL` from January 1, 2010, to January 1, 2020. Finally, we run the backtest using the `cerebro.run()` method and plot the results using the `cerebro.plot()` method.

Analyzing the Backtest Results

After running the backtest, you can analyze the results to evaluate the strategy's performance. Backtrader provides several built-in methods to access performance metrics such as total returns, Sharpe ratio, drawdown, and more.

For example, you can access the total returns of the strategy by adding the following code after running the backtest:

```python
print(f'Total Returns: {cerebro.broker.getvalue()}')
```

You can also access other performance metrics such as the Sharpe ratio and drawdown by using the `cerebro.analyzers.SharpeRatio` and `cerebro.analyzers.DrawDown` classes, respectively. Optimizing the Strategy Parameters One of the key advantages of backtesting in Python is the ability to optimize strategy parameters to improve performance. You can use the `Cerebro` instance's `optstrategy` method to run multiple backtests with different parameter values and compare the results.

Here is an example of how to optimize the `sma1` and `sma2` parameters of the moving average crossover strategy:

```python
for sma1 in range(10, 100, 10):
    for sma2 in range(100, 300, 10):
        cerebro.optstrategy(MovingAverageCrossStrategy,
        sma1=sma1, sma2=sma2)
```

In this code snippet, we loop through different values of `sma1` and `sma2` and run a backtest for each combination of parameters. You can then analyze the results to determine the optimal parameter values for the strategy.

Chapter 9: Machine Learning for Predictive Trading

Machine learning has revolutionized the world of predictive trading by enabling traders to make more informed decisions based on data-driven insights. In this chapter, we will explore how machine learning algorithms can be used to predict stock prices, identify trading opportunities, and optimize trading strategies.

Predictive trading involves using historical data to forecast future price movements and make profitable trades. Machine learning algorithms can analyze large amounts of data to identify patterns and trends that may not be apparent to human traders. By training these algorithms on historical market data, traders can create predictive models that can help them make more accurate predictions about future price movements.

One of the most popular machine learning techniques used in predictive trading is supervised learning. This involves training a model on historical data where the outcome is known, such as stock prices or trading signals. The model can then be used to predict future outcomes based on new data. For example, a supervised learning algorithm could be trained to predict whether a stock price will increase or decrease based on factors such as trading volume, price trends, and market sentiment.

Another common machine learning technique used in predictive trading is reinforcement learning. This involves training a model to make decisions based on feedback from the environment, such as profit or loss on trades. By optimizing for long-term profitability, reinforcement learning algorithms can learn to make better trading decisions over time.

In addition to predicting stock prices, machine learning can also be used to identify trading opportunities and optimize trading strategies. For example, clustering algorithms can group stocks with similar price movements, making it easier to identify potential trading pairs. Sentiment analysis algorithms can analyze news articles and social media posts to gauge market sentiment and identify potential trading opportunities.

Machine learning can also be used to optimize trading strategies by analyzing historical data and identifying patterns that lead to profitable trades. For example, a machine learning algorithm could be trained to identify optimal entry and exit points for trades based on historical price movements. By backtesting these strategies on historical data, traders can evaluate their performance and make adjustments to improve profitability.

Overall, machine learning has the potential to revolutionize the world of predictive trading by enabling traders to make more informed decisions based on data-driven insights. By leveraging machine learning algorithms to predict stock prices, identify trading opportunities, and optimize trading strategies, traders can gain a competitive edge in the market and increase their chances of success.

Introduction to Machine Learning in Finance

Machine learning has revolutionized the way businesses operate in various industries, including finance. In recent years, the financial sector has increasingly adopted machine learning techniques to improve decision- making processes, increase efficiency, and reduce risks. This field, known as machine learning in finance, combines the principles of finance with the power of artificial intelligence to analyze large amounts of data and make predictions or recommendations.

Machine learning in finance involves the use of algorithms and statistical models to analyze financial data, identify patterns, and make predictions. These algorithms are trained on historical data to learn from past trends and patterns, and then applied to new data to make predictions about future outcomes. By leveraging machine learning techniques, financial institutions can make more informed decisions, reduce risks, and improve overall performance.

One of the key applications of machine learning in finance is in the field of algorithmic trading. Algorithmic trading involves the use of computer algorithms to execute trades in financial markets at high speeds and with high frequency. Machine learning algorithms can analyze market data, identify trading opportunities, and execute trades automatically, without human intervention. This can help financial institutions to take advantage of market inefficiencies, reduce trading costs, and increase profitability.

Another important application of machine learning in finance is in the field of credit scoring. Traditional credit scoring models rely on a limited set of variables, such as credit history and income, to assess the creditworthiness of borrowers. Machine learning algorithms, on the other hand, can analyze a wide range of data sources, including social media activity, online shopping behavior, and mobile phone usage, to build more accurate and personalized credit scoring models. This can help financial institutions to better assess the credit risk of borrowers, reduce default rates, and increase lending volumes.

Machine learning is also being used in the field of risk management in finance. By analyzing historical data and identifying patterns and trends, machine learning algorithms can help financial institutions to better understand and quantify risks, such as credit risk, market risk, and operational risk. This can help institutions to develop more effective risk management strategies, reduce losses, and comply with regulatory requirements.

In addition to algorithmic trading, credit scoring, and risk management, machine learning is also being used in other areas of finance, such as fraud detection, customer segmentation, and portfolio management. By leveraging machine learning techniques, financial institutions can gain valuable insights from large amounts of data, make more accurate predictions, and improve decision-making processes.

However, while machine learning offers numerous benefits for the financial sector, it also presents challenges and risks. One of the key challenges is the need for high-quality data. Machine learning algorithms require large amounts of data to learn from, and the quality of the data can significantly impact the accuracy and reliability of the predictions. Financial institutions need to ensure that the data used for training machine learning models is accurate, reliable, and up-to-date.

Another challenge is the interpretability of machine learning models. Many machine learning algorithms are complex and difficult to interpret, making it challenging for financial institutions to understand how the models make predictions. This lack of transparency can raise concerns about bias, discrimination, and regulatory compliance. Financial institutions need to develop methods to explain and interpret machine learning models, in order to build trust and confidence in their predictions.

Despite these challenges, the potential benefits of machine learning in finance are significant. By leveraging the power of artificial intelligence, financial institutions can gain valuable insights, improve decision-making processes, and drive innovation in the industry. Machine learning in finance is a rapidly evolving field, and financial institutions that embrace this technology are likely to gain a competitive advantage in the market.

Machine learning is transforming the financial sector by enabling institutions to analyze large amounts of data, make predictions, and improve decision-making processes. By leveraging machine learning techniques, financial institutions can gain valuable insights, reduce risks, and increase efficiency.

While there are challenges and risks associated with machine learning in finance, the potential benefits are significant. Financial institutions that embrace machine learning are likely to gain a competitive advantage in the market and drive innovation in the industry.

Using Machine Learning Algorithms for Trading Predictions with python

Machine learning algorithms have been increasingly used in the financial industry for making trading predictions. These algorithms can analyze large amounts of data, identify patterns, and make predictions based on historical data. In this article, we will discuss how to use machine learning algorithms for trading predictions with Python.

Python is a popular programming language for data analysis and machine learning. It has a rich ecosystem of libraries and tools that make it easy to work with large datasets and build machine learning models. In this article, we will use Python to implement machine learning algorithms for trading predictions.

To get started, we first need to install the necessary libraries. We will be using the following libraries:

Pandas: A powerful data manipulation library
NumPy: A library for numerical computing
Scikit-learn: A machine learning library
Matplotlib: A library for data visualization

You can install these libraries using pip, the Python package manager. Simply run the following command in your terminal:

```
pip install pandas numpy scikit-learn matplotlib
```

110

Once you have installed the necessary libraries, you can start building your machine learning model. In this example, we will use a simple linear regression model to make trading predictions. Linear regression is a popular machine learning algorithm that can be used to predict continuous values based on input features.

First, let's import the necessary libraries and load the data. For this example, we will use historical stock price data from a CSV file. You can download the sample data file from [link to data file].

```python
import pandas as pdimport numpy as np
from sklearn.linear_model import LinearRegression
import matplotlib.pyplot as plt

# Load the data
data = pd.read_csv('stock_data.csv')

# Display the first few rows of the dataprint(data.head())
```

Next, we need to preprocess the data before building the machine learning model. We will split the data intoinput features and target variables, and then split the data into training and testing sets.

```python
# Split the data into input features and target variableX = data.drop('Close', axis=1)
```

111

```
y = data['Close']

# Split the data into training and testing sets
from sklearn.model_selection import train_test_split
X_train, X_test, y_train, y_test = train_test_split(X, y,
test_size=0.2, random_state=42)
```

Now, we can build the linear regression model and train it on the training data.

```python
# Build the linear regression model model =
LinearRegression()

# Train the model on the training datamodel.fit(X_train,
y_train)
```

Once the model is trained, we can make predictions on the testing data and evaluate the model's performance.

```python
# Make predictions on the testing data predictions =
model.predict(X_test)

# Evaluate the model's performance
from sklearn.metrics import mean_squared_errormse =
mean_squared_error(y_test, predictions) print('Mean
Squared Error:', mse)
```

Finally, we can visualize the model's predictions by

plotting the actual stock prices against the predicted prices.

```python
# Plot the actual and predicted stock prices
plt.figure(figsize=(10, 6))
plt.scatter(y_test.index, y_test, color='blue', label='Actual') plt.scatter(y_test.index, predictions, color='red', label='Predicted')plt.legend()
plt.xlabel('Date') plt.ylabel('Stock Price')
plt.title('Actual vs. Predicted Stock Prices')plt.show()
```

In this example, we used a simple linear regression model to make trading predictions. However, there are many other machine learning algorithms that can be used for trading predictions, such as decision trees, random forests, and support vector machines. You can experiment with different algorithms and hyperparameters to improve the model's performance.

It is important to note that trading predictions are inherently risky and should be used with caution. Machine learning algorithms can help identify patterns in historical data, but they cannot predict future market conditions with certainty. It is always recommended to consult with a financial advisor before making any trading decisions.

Using machine learning algorithms for trading predictions can be a powerful tool for investors and traders. Python's rich ecosystem of libraries and tools make it easy to implement machine learning models for trading predictions. By following the steps outlined in this article, you can build and evaluate machine learning models for

113

trading predictions with Python.

Chapter 10: Sentiment Analysis for Cryptocurrency Markets

Sentiment analysis has become an increasingly important tool for understanding the behavior of cryptocurrency markets. In Chapter 10 of our book, we delve into the intricacies of sentiment analysis for cryptocurrency markets and how it can be used to make informed trading decisions.

Cryptocurrencies have gained significant attention in recent years, with many investors flocking to this new asset class in search of high returns. However, the volatile nature of cryptocurrency markets can make it difficult to predict price movements, leading to increased risk for investors. This is where sentiment analysis comes into play.

Sentiment analysis involves using natural language processing and machine learning techniques to analyze the sentiment of market participants towards a particular cryptocurrency. By analyzing social media posts, news articles, and other sources of information, sentiment analysis can provide valuable insights into the mood of the market and help investors make more informed trading decisions.

One of the key challenges of sentiment analysis for cryptocurrency markets is the sheer volume of data that needs to be analyzed. With thousands of social media posts and news articles being published every day, it can be difficult to separate the signal from the noise. This is where machine learning algorithms come into play, helping to identify patterns in the data and extract meaningful insights.

In Chapter 10, we discuss the various approaches to sentiment analysis for cryptocurrency markets, including lexicon-based methods, machine learning models, and deep learning techniques. We also explore the challenges and limitations of sentiment analysis, such as the inherent subjectivity of language and the difficulty of accurately capturing the nuances of human emotions.

Despite these challenges, sentiment analysis has proven to be a valuable tool for understanding cryptocurrency markets. By analyzing the sentiment of market participants, investors can gain valuable insights into market trends and make more informed trading decisions. For example, a sudden spike in positive sentiment towards aparticular cryptocurrency could indicate a potential price increase, while a surge in negative sentiment could signal a looming downturn.

In addition to helping investors make better trading decisions, sentiment analysis can also be used to monitor market sentiment over time and identify emerging trends. By tracking changes in sentiment towards a particular cryptocurrency, investors can stay ahead of the curve and adjust their trading strategies accordingly.

Overall, sentiment analysis is a powerful tool for understanding cryptocurrency markets and making informedtrading decisions. By analyzing the sentiment of market participants, investors can gain valuable insights into market trends and identify potential opportunities for profit. In Chapter 10 of our book, we provide a comprehensive overview of sentiment analysis for cryptocurrency markets and discuss the various approaches and techniques that can be used to analyze market sentiment.

Understanding Sentiment Analysis in Cryptocurrency Markets

Sentiment analysis is a powerful tool that can be used to understand the emotions and opinions of individuals in the cryptocurrency market. By analyzing and interpreting the sentiment of investors and traders, it is possible to gain valuable insights into market trends and make more informed investment decisions.

In the world of cryptocurrency, where prices can be highly volatile and influenced by a wide range of factors, sentiment analysis can provide a valuable edge for investors looking to navigate the market. By understanding the emotions and opinions of market participants, it is possible to anticipate price movements and identify potential opportunities for profit.

There are a number of different methods that can be used to analyze sentiment in the cryptocurrency market. One common approach is to use natural language processing (NLP) techniques to analyze social media posts, news articles, and other sources of information for sentiment indicators. By analyzing the language used in these sources, it is possible to gauge the overall sentiment of the market and identify trends and patterns that may impact prices.

Another approach to sentiment analysis in the cryptocurrency market is to use machine learning algorithms to analyze market data and identify patterns that may indicate sentiment. By training these algorithms on historical data, it is possible to predict future price movements based on sentiment indicators.

One of the key challenges of sentiment analysis in the cryptocurrency market is the sheer volume of data that must be analyzed. With millions of social media posts, news articles, and other sources of information being generated every day, it can be difficult to sift through this data and identify meaningful sentiment indicators. However, by using advanced data analytics techniques and machine learning algorithms, it is possible to automate this process and identify sentiment indicators in real-time.

One of the key benefits of sentiment analysis in the cryptocurrency market is its ability to provide early warning signs of market trends. By analyzing sentiment indicators, it is possible to identify potential market movements before they occur, giving investors an opportunity to position themselves accordingly. For example, if sentiment indicators suggest that investors are becoming increasingly bullish on a particular cryptocurrency, it may be a signal that prices are likely to rise in the near future.

In addition to providing early warning signs of market trends, sentiment analysis can also help investors to gauge the overall mood of the market. By understanding the emotions and opinions of market participants, it is possible to assess the level of risk in the market and make more informed decisions about when to buy or sell cryptocurrencies. For example, if sentiment indicators suggest that investors are becoming increasingly bearish on a particular cryptocurrency, it may be a signal that prices are likely to fall in the near future.

Overall, sentiment analysis is a valuable tool for investors looking to navigate the cryptocurrency market. By analyzing the emotions and opinions of market participants, it is possible to gain valuable insights into market trends and make more informed investment decisions.

Whether using natural language processing techniques or machine learning algorithms, sentiment analysis can provide a competitive edge for investors looking to succeed in the fast-paced world of cryptocurrency trading.

Implementing Sentiment Analysis with Python - scripts

Sentiment analysis is a powerful tool that allows us to understand the emotions and opinions expressed in text data. By using natural language processing techniques, we can analyze the sentiment of a piece of text and determine whether the overall sentiment is positive, negative, or neutral. In this article, we will explore how to implement sentiment analysis with Python using scripts and examples.

To get started with sentiment analysis in Python, we first need to install the necessary libraries. The most popular library for natural language processing in Python is NLTK (Natural Language Toolkit). We can install NLTK using pip by running the following command:

```
pip install nltk
```

Once NLTK is installed, we can import the library and download the necessary resources for sentiment analysis. NLTK provides a built-in dataset called VADER (Valence Aware Dictionary and sEntiment Reasoner) that can be used for sentiment analysis. We can download the VADER lexicon by running the following code:

```python
import nltk
nltk.download('vader_lexicon')
```

Now that we have the necessary resources, we can start implementing sentiment analysis with Python. Let's create a simple script that analyzes the sentiment of a given text using the VADER lexicon. Here is an examplescript:

```python
from                nltk.sentiment.vader               import
SentimentIntensityAnalyzer

# Create a SentimentIntensityAnalyzer object sid =
SentimentIntensityAnalyzer()

# Define a function to analyze the sentiment of a given text
def analyze_sentiment(text):
sentiment_score     =     sid.polarity_scores(text)     if
sentiment_score['compound'] >= 0.05: return 'Positive'
elif  sentiment_score['compound']   <=   -0.05:  return
'Negative'
else:
return 'Neutral'

# Test the function with a sample texttext = "I love Python
programming!"sentiment = analyze_sentiment(text)
```

```
print(f"The sentiment of the text '{text}' is {sentiment}")
```

In this script, we first import the `SentimentIntensityAnalyzer` class from the NLTK library. We then create an instance of the `SentimentIntensityAnalyzer` class and define a function called `analyze_sentiment` that takes a text input and returns the sentiment of the text as either 'Positive', 'Negative', or 'Neutral' based on the compoundsentiment score.

Next, we test the `analyze_sentiment` function with a sample text ("I love Python programming!") and print the sentiment of the text. When we run the script, we should see the output:

```
The sentiment of the text 'I love Python programming!' is Positive
```

This example demonstrates how to perform sentiment analysis on a single piece of text. However, in real-world applications, we often need to analyze the sentiment of multiple texts in a more efficient manner. To do this, we can read a dataset containing text data and analyze the sentiment of each text in the dataset.

Let's create another script that reads a CSV file containing text data and analyzes the sentiment of each textusing the VADER lexicon. Here is an example script:

```python
import pandas as pd
from            nltk.sentiment.vader            import
SentimentIntensityAnalyzer

# Load the dataset
data = pd.read_csv('data.csv')

# Create a SentimentIntensityAnalyzer object sid =
SentimentIntensityAnalyzer()

# Define a function to analyze the sentiment of a given text
def analyze_sentiment(text):
sentiment_score    =    sid.polarity_scores(text)    if
sentiment_score['compound'] >= 0.05: return 'Positive'
elif sentiment_score['compound'] <= -0.05: return
'Negative'
else:
return 'Neutral'

# Analyze the sentiment of each text in the dataset
data['Sentiment'] = data['Text'].apply(analyze_sentiment)

# Save the results to a new CSV file
data.to_csv('sentiment_analysis_results.csv',    index=False)
```

```

```

In this script, we first import the `pandas` library to load the dataset from a CSV file. We then load the dataset using the `pd.read_csv` function and create an instance of the `SentimentIntensityAnalyzer` class.

Next, we define the `analyze_sentiment` function, which takes a text input and returns the sentiment of the text as either 'Positive', 'Negative', or 'Neutral' based on the compound sentiment score. We then apply the `analyze_sentiment` function to each text in the dataset using the `apply` method and store the results in a new column called 'Sentiment'.

Finally, we save the results to a new CSV file called 'sentiment_analysis_results.csv' using the `to_csv` method.

By running this script with a dataset containing text data, we can perform sentiment analysis on multiple texts and save the results to a new CSV file. This allows us to analyze the sentiment of a large amount of text

Chapter 11: Algorithmic Trading Strategies

Algorithmic trading has become increasingly popular in the financial markets due to its ability to execute trades at high speeds and with precision. In this chapter, we will explore some of the most common algorithmic trading strategies used by traders and institutions to generate profits in the markets.

One of the most popular algorithmic trading strategies is trend following. This strategy involves identifying the direction of a market trend and then entering trades in the direction of that trend.

Traders use technical indicators such as moving averages, MACD, and RSI to identify trends and determine entry and exit points for their trades. Trend following strategies are popular because they can be highly profitable in trending markets, where prices tend to move in one direction for an extended period of time.

Another common algorithmic trading strategy is mean reversion. This strategy involves identifying overbought or oversold conditions in a market and then entering trades in the opposite direction in anticipation of a price correction. Traders use statistical tools such as Bollinger Bands, stochastic oscillators, and RSI to identify mean reversion opportunities and determine entry and exit points for their trades. Mean reversion strategies can be profitable in range-bound markets, where prices tend to oscillate between support and resistance levels.

Arbitrage is another popular algorithmic trading strategy that involves exploiting price differentials between different markets or assets. Traders use sophisticated algorithms to identify arbitrage opportunities and execute trades to profit from these price differences. Arbitrage strategies can be highly profitable but also carry a high level of risk, as markets can move quickly and erode profits if trades are not executed in a timely manner.

Pairs trading is a strategy that involves trading two correlated assets simultaneously in order to profit from the relative price movements between them. Traders identify pairs of assets that have a strong historical correlation and then enter trades when the price relationship between the two assets diverges from its historical average.
Pairs trading strategies can be profitable in markets where assets are highly correlated, such as stocks in the same sector or commodities with a strong fundamental relationship.

Machine learning and artificial intelligence are increasingly being used in algorithmic trading strategies to analyze large amounts of data and identify profitable trading opportunities. These technologies can analyze market data in real-time and make trading decisions based on historical patterns and market conditions. Machine learning algorithms can adapt to changing market conditions and learn from past trades to improve their performance over time.

In conclusion, algorithmic trading strategies are an essential tool for traders and institutions looking to generate profits in the financial markets. By using sophisticated algorithms and advanced technologies, traders can execute trades at high speeds and with precision, allowing them to take advantage of profitable trading opportunities in a fast-paced and competitive market environment. Whether you are a novice trader or an experienced professional, algorithmic trading strategies can help you achieve your financial goals and maximize your trading profits.

Algorithmic Trading Fundamentals

Algorithmic trading is a method of executing trades using automated pre-programmed trading instructions. These instructions are based on a set of rules and criteria that are determined by the trader or investor.
Algorithmic trading is also known as algo trading or black-box trading.

Algorithmic trading can be used in a variety of financial markets, including stocks, futures, options, and currencies. It has become increasingly popular in recent years due to advancements in technology and the availability of high-speed internet connections.

There are several key components to algorithmic trading. These include the development of trading strategies, the backtesting of those strategies, and the implementation of the strategies in a live trading environment.

Developing a trading strategy involves identifying patterns in market data and determining how to exploit those patterns for profit. This can involve technical analysis, fundamental analysis, or a combination of both. Traders may also use machine learning algorithms to help identify profitable trading opportunities.

Once a trading strategy has been developed, it must be backtested to ensure that it is profitable over a historical period of time. Backtesting involves running the strategy on historical market data to see how it would have performed in the past. This helps traders identify any weaknesses in the strategy and make adjustments as needed.

After a trading strategy has been successfully backtested, it can be implemented in a live trading environment. This involves connecting the trading algorithm to a brokerage account and allowing it to execute trades automatically based on the predefined rules and criteria.

There are several advantages to algorithmic trading. One of the main benefits is the ability to execute trades at high speeds. Algorithms can analyze market data and execute trades much faster than a human trader, which can be crucial in fast-moving markets.

Algorithmic trading also allows traders to take emotion out of the trading process. Emotions such as fear and greed can cloud judgment and lead to poor trading decisions. By using automated trading algorithms, traders can stick to their predefined rules and criteria without being swayed by emotions.

Another advantage of algorithmic trading is the ability to backtest trading strategies. This allows traders to see how a strategy would have performed in the past and make adjustments as needed. Backtesting can help traders identify profitable trading opportunities and avoid costly mistakes.

Despite its advantages, algorithmic trading also has some drawbacks. One of the main risks is the potential for technical glitches or system failures. If a trading algorithm malfunctions or encounters a technical issue, it can lead to significant losses for the trader.

Algorithmic trading can also be complex and difficult to understand for beginners. Developing profitable trading strategies requires a deep understanding of market dynamics and technical analysis. Traders may need to invest time and resources in learning how to develop and implement successful trading algorithms.

Algorithmic trading is a powerful tool that can help traders execute trades more efficiently and profitably. By developing and backtesting trading strategies, traders can identify profitable trading opportunities and automate their trading process.

However, algorithmic trading also comes with risks and challenges that traders must be aware of. Overall, algorithmic trading can be a valuable tool for traders looking to improve their trading performance and take advantage of market opportunities.

Developing and Testing Algorithmic Strategies

Developing and testing algorithmic strategies in language is a crucial aspect of natural language processing and computational linguistics. Algorithms are the backbone of any language processing system, as they determine how the system will interpret and generate language. In this article, we will explore the process of developing and testing algorithmic strategies in language, and discuss some best practices for ensuring the accuracy and efficiency of these algorithms.

The first step in developing algorithmic strategies for language processing is to define the problem that needs to be solved. This could involve tasks such as text classification, sentiment analysis, machine translation, or speech recognition. Once the problem has been defined, the next step is to research existing algorithms and techniques that have been used to address similar problems in the past. This research will help to inform the design of the new algorithm and ensure that it is based on sound principles.

After researching existing algorithms, the next step is to design a new algorithm that is tailored to the specific problem at hand. This may involve combining elements of existing algorithms, or developing entirely new techniques. The algorithm should be designed to be efficient, accurate, and scalable, so that it can handle large amounts of language data in real-time.

Once the algorithm has been designed, the next step is to

implement it in a programming language such as Python, Java, or C++. The implementation should be thoroughly tested to ensure that it is functioning correctly and producing accurate results. This testing process may involve running the algorithm on sample language data sets, comparing its output to known correct results, and debugging any errors that are found.

In addition to testing the algorithm for correctness, it is also important to test it for efficiency. This involves measuring the algorithm's performance in terms of speed and memory usage, and optimizing it to ensure that it can handle large language data sets in a reasonable amount of time. This may involve making changes to the algorithm's design, or implementing parallel processing techniques to speed up its execution.

Once the algorithm has been developed and tested, the next step is to evaluate its performance on real-world language data. This may involve running the algorithm on a large corpus of text, and comparing its output to human-generated annotations or other ground truth data. This evaluation process will help to determine how well the algorithm performs in practice, and whether any further refinements are needed.

In addition to evaluating the algorithm's performance, it is also important to consider its ethical implications. Language processing algorithms have the potential to impact individuals and communities in significant ways, so it is important to ensure that they are fair, transparent, and unbiased. This may involve testing the algorithm on diverse language data sets to ensure that it does not exhibit bias or discrimination, and implementing safeguards to protect user privacy and data security.

Overall, developing and testing algorithmic strategies in language is a complex and challenging process that requires careful planning, research, and implementation. By following best practices and conducting thorough testing, developers can ensure that their algorithms are accurate, efficient, and ethical, and can make a positive impact on the field of natural language processing.

Chapter 12: Risk Management in Cryptocurrency Trading

Risk management is a crucial aspect of cryptocurrency trading. With the volatile nature of the market and the potential for significant gains or losses, it is essential for traders to have a solid risk management strategy in place to protect their investments and minimize potential losses.

There are several key principles that traders should keep in mind when it comes to risk management in cryptocurrency trading. These include diversification, setting stop-loss orders, managing leverage, and staying informed about market trends and developments.

Diversification is a fundamental risk management strategy that involves spreading your investments across different assets to reduce the impact of any single asset's performance on your overall portfolio. By diversifying your investments, you can minimize the risk of losing all your capital if one asset performs poorly.

Setting stop-loss orders is another critical risk management tool that traders can use to protect their investments. A stop-loss order is a predetermined price at which a trader will sell their asset to limit their losses. By setting stop-loss orders, traders can ensure that they do not incur significant losses if the market moves against them.

Managing leverage is also essential when it comes to risk management in cryptocurrency trading. Leverage allows traders to amplify their potential gains, but it also increases the risk of significant losses. It is crucial for traders to use leverage carefully and not overextend themselves to avoid potential liquidation of their positions.

Staying informed about market trends and developments is another key aspect of risk management in cryptocurrency trading. By staying up to date with the latest news and developments in the market, traders can make informed decisions about their investments and adjust their strategies accordingly to minimize potential risks.

In addition to these key principles, there are several risk management tools that traders can use to protect their investments and minimize potential losses. These include risk management software, risk assessment tools, and risk management frameworks.

Risk management software can help traders track their investments, set stop-loss orders, and manage their portfolios effectively. By using risk management software, traders can automate many aspects of their risk management strategy and ensure that they are always protected from potential losses.

Risk assessment tools can also be valuable for traders looking to assess the potential risks associated with their investments. By using risk assessment tools, traders can identify potential risks and develop strategies to mitigate them effectively.

Risk management frameworks provide traders with a structured approach to managing risk in their cryptocurrency trading activities. By following a risk management framework, traders can ensure that they are taking a systematic approach to managing risk and protecting their investments.

Risk management is a crucial aspect of cryptocurrency trading that all traders should prioritize. By following key principles such as diversification, setting stop-loss orders, managing leverage, and staying informed about market trends, traders can protect their investments and minimize potential losses effectively.

By using risk management tools such as risk management software, risk assessment tools, and risk management frameworks, traders can further enhance their risk management strategies and ensure that they are well-prepared to navigate the volatile cryptocurrency market.

Understanding Risk in Trading

Understanding risk in trading is a crucial aspect of becoming a successful trader. Risk is an inherent part of trading and cannot be eliminated entirely. However, by understanding and managing risk effectively, traders can increase their chances of success and minimize potential losses.

Risk in trading refers to the possibility of losing money on a trade. There are various types of risks that tradersneed to be aware of, including market risk, credit risk, liquidity risk, and operational risk. Each type of risk can have a significant impact on a trader's portfolio and overall trading performance.

Market risk is the most common type of risk in trading and refers to the possibility of losing money due to changes in the market. Market risk can be caused by various factors, including economic events, geopolitical events, and market sentiment. Traders need to be aware of market risk and take steps to manage it effectively,such as using stop-loss orders and diversifying their portfolios.

Credit risk is another important type of risk in trading, which refers to the possibility of losing money due to the default of a counterparty. Credit risk can occur when trading with brokers, exchanges, or other traders. Traders need to assess the creditworthiness of their counterparties and take steps to mitigate credit risk, such as using reputable brokers and exchanges.

Liquidity risk is the risk of not being able to buy or sell an asset at a desired price. Liquidity risk can occur when trading in illiquid markets or assets. Traders need to be aware of liquidity risk and take steps to manage it effectively, such as trading in liquid markets and assets.

Operational risk is the risk of losses due to human error, system failures, or other operational issues. Operational risk can have a significant impact on a trader's performance and profitability. Traders need to implement robust risk management processes and procedures to mitigate operational risk effectively.

To manage risk effectively in trading, traders need to adopt a risk management strategy that suits their trading style and risk tolerance. Some common risk management techniques include setting stop-loss orders, diversifying portfolios, using leverage cautiously, and implementing risk-reward ratios.

Stop-loss orders are an essential tool for managing risk in trading. A stop-loss order is an order placed with a broker to buy or sell a security once it reaches a certain price. By using stop-loss orders, traders can limit their losses and protect their capital from significant declines.

Diversification is another crucial risk management technique in trading. Diversification involves spreading investments across different assets, markets, and sectors to reduce the impact of market risk on a trader's portfolio. By diversifying their portfolios, traders can minimize the risk of significant losses from a single trade or asset.

Using leverage cautiously is essential for managing risk in trading. Leverage allows traders to control larger positions with a smaller amount of capital. While leverage can amplify profits, it can also increase losses significantly. Traders need to use leverage cautiously and avoid overleveraging their positions to manage risk effectively.

Implementing risk-reward ratios is another important risk management technique in trading. A risk-reward ratio is a measure of the potential reward of a trade compared to its potential risk. By using risk-reward ratios, traders can assess the potential profitability of a trade and make informed decisions about whether to enter a trade.

Understanding risk in trading is essential for becoming a successful trader. By being aware of the various types of risks in trading and implementing effective risk management techniques, traders can increase their chances of success and minimize potential losses. Risk is an inherent part of trading, but by managing risk effectively, traders can achieve their trading goals and objectives.

Implementing Risk Management Techniques with python - scripts

Risk management is a crucial aspect of any business or project. It involves identifying, assessing, and mitigating risks that could potentially impact the success of the endeavor. By implementing risk management techniques, organizations can proactively address potential issues and minimize their impact on the project.

One effective way to implement risk management techniques is through the use of Python scripts. Python is a versatile and powerful programming language that is widely used in various industries for data analysis, automation, and more. By leveraging Python scripts, organizations can automate the process of identifying and managing risks, making the risk management process more efficient and effective.

In this article, we will explore how to implement risk management techniques using Python scripts. We will provide examples of Python scripts that can be used to identify, assess, and mitigate risks in a project or business. By the end of this article, you will have a better understanding of how Python scripts can be used to enhance risk management practices.

Identifying Risks with Python Scripts

The first step in effective risk management is to identify potential risks that could impact the project or business. This involves analyzing various factors such as project scope, timelines, resources, and more to identifypotential threats. Python scripts can be used to automate the process of identifying risks by analyzing data and generating risk reports.

For example, a Python script can be used to analyze project data and identify potential risks based on historical data and project parameters. The script can scan through project documents, timelines, and resource allocations to identify potential risks such as budget overruns, delays, resource shortages, and more. By automating the process of risk identification, organizations can save time and resources while ensuring that all potential risks areconsidered.

Assessing Risks with Python Scripts

Once potential risks have been identified, the next step is to assess the likelihood and impact of each risk. This involves analyzing the probability of each risk occurring and the potential impact it could have on the project or business. Python scripts can be used to automate the process of risk assessment by calculating risk scores based on various factors.

For example, a Python script can be used to calculate risk scores for each identified risk based on factors such as likelihood, impact, and severity. The script can assign a numerical value to each risk based on these factors, allowing organizations to prioritize risks based on their potential impact. By automating the process of risk assessment, organizations can make informed decisions about which risks to focus on and how to allocate resources for risk mitigation.

Mitigating Risks with Python Scripts

Once risks have been identified and assessed, the next step is to develop a risk mitigation strategy to address potential threats. This involves implementing measures to reduce the likelihood and impact of risks, as well as developing contingency plans to address risks if they occur. Python scripts can be used to automate the process of risk mitigation by generating risk mitigation plans and monitoring risk mitigation efforts.

For example, a Python script can be used to generate risk mitigation plans for each identified risk based on the risk assessment scores. The script can outline specific actions that need to be taken to reduce the likelihood and impact of each risk, as well as contingency plans to address risks if they occur. By automating the process of risk mitigation, organizations can ensure that all potential threats are addressed and that resources are allocated effectively.

Monitoring Risks with Python Scripts

Once risk mitigation plans have been implemented, it is important to monitor risks to ensure that they are effectively managed. This involves tracking the progress of risk mitigation efforts, monitoring changes in risk factors, and adjusting risk mitigation plans as needed. Python scripts can be used to automate the process of risk monitoring by analyzing data and generating risk monitoring reports.

For example, a Python script can be used to monitor changes in risk factors such as project timelines, resource allocations, and budget allocations. The script can analyze data in real-time to identify any changes that could impact the likelihood and impact of risks. By automating the process of risk monitoring, organizations can proactively address potential issues and ensure that risk mitigation efforts are effective.

Implementing risk management techniques with Python scripts can enhance the effectiveness of risk management practices in organizations. By automating the process of risk identification, assessment, mitigation, and monitoring, organizations can proactively address potential threats and minimize their impact on projects or businesses. Python scripts can streamline the risk management process, saving time and resources while ensuring that all potential risks are considered and addressed.

By leveraging the power of Python scripts, organizations can enhance their risk management practices and improve the success of their projects or businesses. Whether you are a project manager, business owner, or risk management professional, implementing risk management techniques with Python scripts can help you effectively manage risks and achieve your goals.

Chapter 13: Portfolio Management and Diversification

Portfolio management is a crucial aspect of investing that involves the selection and maintenance of a group of investments that collectively make up an individual's investment portfolio. The goal of portfolio management is to maximize returns while minimizing risk through diversification. Diversification is the practice of spreading investments across different asset classes, industries, and geographic regions to reduce the impact of any single investment on the overall portfolio.

Diversification is based on the principle that different types of investments tend to perform differently under various market conditions. By diversifying a portfolio, an investor can reduce the risk of significant losses from any one investment. For example, if a portfolio is heavily weighted in one industry and that industry experiences a downturn, the entire portfolio could suffer. However, if the portfolio is diversified across multiple industries, the impact of the downturn on the overall portfolio would be less severe.

There are several key benefits to diversification. First and foremost, diversification helps to reduce risk. By spreading investments across different asset classes, industries, and geographic regions, investors can minimize the impact of market fluctuations on their portfolio. This can help to protect against significant losses and preserve capital over the long term.

Diversification also helps to improve the risk-adjusted return of a portfolio. By including a mix of investments with different risk profiles, investors can potentially achieve higher returns for a given level of risk. This is known as the efficient frontier, which represents the optimal combination of risk and return for a given portfolio.

In addition, diversification can help to smooth out the volatility of a portfolio. By including investments that are negatively correlated with each other, such as stocks and bonds, investors can reduce the overall volatility of their portfolio. This can help to provide more stable returns over time and reduce the emotional impact of market fluctuations.

There are several different ways to diversify a portfolio. One common approach is to invest in a mix of asset classes, such as stocks, bonds, and cash equivalents. Each asset class has its own risk and return characteristics, so by including a mix of assets, investors can achieve a more balanced portfolio.

Another approach to diversification is to invest in different industries and sectors. By spreading investments across industries such as technology, healthcare, and consumer goods, investors can reduce the impact of any single industry on the overall portfolio. This can help to protect against industry-specific risks and provide more stable returns over time.

Geographic diversification is also important for reducing

risk. By investing in different regions around the world, investors can reduce the impact of political, economic, and currency risks on their portfolio. This canhelp to provide more stable returns and protect against global market fluctuations.

Overall, portfolio management and diversification are essential components of a successful investment strategy. By carefully selecting and maintaining a diversified portfolio, investors can maximize returns while minimizingrisk.

Diversification helps to reduce the impact of market fluctuations, improve the risk-adjusted return of a portfolio, and smooth out volatility. By following these principles, investors can build a strong and resilientportfolio that can withstand the ups and downs of the market.

Portfolio Management Market Making in Trading

Portfolio management and market making are two key components of the trading industry that play a crucial role in ensuring the success of investors and financial institutions. In this article, we will explore the concepts of portfolio management and market making, their importance in the trading world, and how they work together to create a successful trading strategy.

Portfolio management is the process of selecting and managing a group of investments that are held by an individual or institution. The goal of portfolio management is to maximize returns while minimizing risk by diversifying investments across different asset classes and industries. Portfolio managers use various strategies and techniques to achieve these objectives, including asset allocation, risk management, and performance evaluation.

Market making, on the other hand, is the process of providing liquidity to financial markets by buying and selling securities on a continuous basis. Market makers play a crucial role in ensuring that there is a smooth flow of trading activity in the market, as they are responsible for maintaining an orderly market and ensuring that there are buyers and sellers for every security.

Market makers make money by profiting from the spread between the bid and ask prices of securities. They buy securities at the bid price and sell them at the ask price, capturing a profit on each transaction. Market makers also provide liquidity by standing ready to buy or sell securities at any time, which helps to reduce volatility in the market and ensures that investors can easily buy or sell securities when they need to.

Portfolio managers and market makers work together to create a successful trading strategy that maximizes returns while minimizing risk. Portfolio managers rely on market makers to provide liquidity to the market, allowing them to buy and sell securities at competitive prices. Market makers, in turn, rely on portfolio managers to provide them with a steady flow of orders to execute, which helps them to generate profits from their trading activities.

One of the key benefits of market making in trading is that it helps to reduce the cost of trading for investors. By providing liquidity to the market, market makers help to ensure that there are always buyers and sellers for securities, which reduces the bid-ask spread and allows investors to buy and sell securities at more competitive prices. This, in turn, helps to lower transaction costs for investors and improves the overall efficiency of the market.

Portfolio managers also benefit from market making by having access to a deep and liquid market for trading their securities. Market makers provide a valuable service by ensuring that there is always a market for securities, which allows portfolio managers to buy and sell securities quickly and efficiently. This helps portfolio managers to implement their trading strategies more effectively and achieve better returns for their clients.

In addition to providing liquidity to the market, market makers also play a crucial role in maintaining market stability and preventing excessive volatility. By standing ready to buy or sell securities at any time, market makers help to smooth out fluctuations in the market and ensure that prices remain stable. This helps to create a more orderly market environment and reduces the risk of sudden price movements that can disrupt trading activity.

Overall, portfolio management and market making are two essential components of the trading industry that work together to create a successful trading strategy.

Portfolio managers rely on market makers to provide liquidity to the market and execute their trades efficiently, while market makers rely on portfolio managers to provide them with a steady flow of orders to execute.

By working together, portfolio managers and market makers can create a more efficient and stable market environment that benefits investors and financial institutions alike.

Strategies for Diversifying Cryptocurrency Investments

In recent years, cryptocurrency has become a popular investment option for many individuals looking to diversify their portfolios. With the rise of Bitcoin and other digital currencies, there are now more opportunities than ever to invest in this emerging asset class. However, like any investment, it is important to have a well-thought-out strategy in place to ensure that you are maximizing your returns while minimizing your risks. In this article, we will explore some strategies for diversifying your cryptocurrency investments to help you build a more robust and resilient portfolio.

Spread your investments across different cryptocurrencies

One of the most basic strategies for diversifying your cryptocurrency investments is to spread your money across different digital assets. This can help reduce your exposure to any one particular cryptocurrency and minimize the impact of a potential crash in the market. By investing in a variety of coins, you can take advantage of the different growth potential and risk profiles of each asset.

When choosing which cryptocurrencies to invest in, it is important to do your research and consider factors such as market capitalization, trading volume, and development team. Look for projects that have strong fundamentals and a clear use case, as these are more likely to withstand market volatility and deliver long-term returns.

Invest in different sectors of the cryptocurrency market

In addition to diversifying across different cryptocurrencies, you can also diversify your investments by sector. The cryptocurrency market is made up of a variety of sectors, including decentralized finance (DeFi), non- fungible tokens (NFTs), and blockchain infrastructure. By investing in a mix of sectors, you can spread your risk and take advantage of different growth opportunities.

For example, if you are bullish on the future of DeFi, you may want to allocate a portion of your portfolio to DeFi tokens such as Uniswap or Aave. If you believe in the potential of NFTs, you could invest in projects like Decentraland or Axie Infinity. By diversifying across sectors, you can capture the upside potential of different trends in the cryptocurrency market.

Consider investing in stablecoins

While most cryptocurrencies are known for their volatility, stablecoins are a type of digital asset that are designed to maintain a stable value. These coins are typically pegged to a fiat currency such as the US dollar or euro, making them less susceptible to price fluctuations. By investing in stablecoins, you can protect your portfolio against market volatility and reduce your overall risk exposure.

Stablecoins can also be used as a hedge against market downturns, as they tend to hold their value during periods of market instability. Additionally, stablecoins can be a useful tool for trading and liquidity management, as they can be easily converted into other cryptocurrencies or fiat currencies.

Utilize dollar-cost averaging

Dollar-cost averaging is a strategy that involves investing a fixed amount of money at regular intervals, regardless of the price of the asset. This approach can help smooth out the impact of market volatility and reduce the risk of making emotional investment decisions based on short-term price movements.

To implement dollar-cost averaging with cryptocurrency, you can set up recurring purchases on a cryptocurrency exchange or use a dollar-cost averaging service. By investing a fixed amount of money each week or month, you can gradually build your cryptocurrency portfolio over time and take advantage of price fluctuations to accumulate more coins at lower prices.

Consider investing in cryptocurrency index funds

For investors looking for a more passive approach to diversifying their cryptocurrency investments, cryptocurrency index funds can be a good option. These funds track the performance of a basket of cryptocurrencies and offer exposure to a diversified portfolio of digital assets. By investing in an index fund, you can gain broad exposure to the cryptocurrency market without having to pick individual coins.

Cryptocurrency index funds are typically managed by professional asset managers who rebalance the portfolio regularly to reflect changes in the market. This can help reduce the risk of concentration in any one particular asset and provide more stable returns over the long term. Some popular cryptocurrency index funds include the Bitwise 10 Crypto Index Fund and the Grayscale Digital Large Cap Fund.

Use risk management techniques

In addition to diversifying your cryptocurrency investments, it is important to implement risk management techniques to protect your portfolio against potential losses. One common risk management strategy is setting stop-loss orders, which automatically sell your assets if they reach a certain price level. This can help limit your losses and prevent you from holding onto a losing position for too long.

Another risk management technique is setting a target allocation for each asset in your portfolio and rebalancing regularly to maintain your desired mix. By periodically adjusting your portfolio to reflect changes in the market, you can ensure that you are not overly exposed to any one particular asset or sector.

Diversifying your cryptocurrency investments is essential for building a resilient and profitable portfolio. By spreading your money across different cryptocurrencies, sectors, and risk management techniques, you can reduce your exposure to market volatility and maximize your returns over the long term. Whether you are a seasoned investor

Chapter 14: Cryptocurrency Arbitrage Opportunities

Cryptocurrency arbitrage is a trading strategy that involves taking advantage of price differences of a cryptocurrency across different exchanges. This strategy allows traders to profit from the inefficiencies in the market and make money with minimal risk. In this chapter, we will explore the various opportunities for cryptocurrency arbitrage and how traders can capitalize on them.

Arbitrage opportunities in the cryptocurrency market arise due to the decentralized nature of the market and the lack of a single global price for cryptocurrencies. Different exchanges may have different prices for the same cryptocurrency due to factors such as supply and demand, liquidity, and trading volume. This creates opportunities for traders to buy low on one exchange and sell high on another, pocketing the price difference as profit.

One of the most common types of cryptocurrency arbitrage is exchange arbitrage, where traders buy a cryptocurrency on one exchange where the price is lower and sell it on another exchange where the price is higher. This can be done manually by monitoring prices on different exchanges and executing trades manually, or automatically using trading bots that are programmed to execute trades based on predefined criteria.

Another type of cryptocurrency arbitrage is triangular

arbitrage, where traders exploit price differences between three different cryptocurrencies to make a profit. This involves trading one cryptocurrency for another, then trading that second cryptocurrency for a third, and finally trading the third cryptocurrency back to the original one. By taking advantage of price differences between the three cryptocurrencies, traders can make a profit without taking on any market risk.

Arbitrage opportunities in the cryptocurrency market can be lucrative, but they also come with risks. One of the main risks of cryptocurrency arbitrage is the volatility of the market. Prices of cryptocurrencies can fluctuate rapidly, and if a trader is not able to execute trades quickly enough, they may miss out on the arbitrage opportunity. Additionally, there is always the risk of exchange hacks, technical issues, or regulatory changes that can impact the profitability of arbitrage trades.

To successfully capitalize on cryptocurrency arbitrage opportunities, traders need to have a good understanding of the market, access to multiple exchanges, and the ability to execute trades quickly and efficiently. They also need to have a solid risk management strategy in place to minimize potential losses. It is important to do thorough research and due diligence before engaging in cryptocurrency arbitrage to ensure that the potential rewards outweigh the risks involved.

Overall, cryptocurrency arbitrage can be a profitable trading strategy for experienced traders who are able to identify and capitalize on opportunities in the market. By leveraging price differences across different exchanges and cryptocurrencies, traders can generate consistent profits with minimal risk. However, it is important to approach cryptocurrency arbitrage with caution and to always be aware of the risks involved. With the right knowledge and skills, traders can take advantage of arbitrage opportunities and maximize their profits in the cryptocurrency market.

Understanding Arbitrage in Cryptocurrency Markets

Arbitrage in cryptocurrency markets is a trading strategy that involves taking advantage of price differences between different exchanges or markets. It is a way for traders to profit from the inefficiencies in the market and can be a lucrative opportunity for those who understand how it works.

To understand arbitrage in cryptocurrency markets, it is important to first understand how cryptocurrencies are traded. Cryptocurrencies are digital assets that can be bought and sold on various online platforms known as exchanges. These exchanges allow users to trade cryptocurrencies for other cryptocurrencies or for fiat currencies such as USD or EUR.

Arbitrage in cryptocurrency markets occurs when the price of a cryptocurrency on one exchange is higher than the price on another exchange. Traders can buy the cryptocurrency at the lower price on one exchange and sell it at the higher price on another exchange, making a profit in the process.

There are several types of arbitrage strategies that traders can use in cryptocurrency markets. One common strategy is known as simple arbitrage, where traders buy and sell the same cryptocurrency on different exchanges simultaneously. Another strategy is known as triangular arbitrage, where traders take advantage of price differences between three different cryptocurrencies to make a profit.

Arbitrage in cryptocurrency markets can be a risky strategy, as prices can change rapidly and there is always the risk of losing money. However, for those who understand how the market works and are able to execute tradesquickly, arbitrage can be a profitable opportunity.

One of the key factors to consider when engaging in arbitrage in cryptocurrency markets is the fees charged by exchanges. Some exchanges charge higher fees than others, which can eat into profits made through arbitrage. Traders should carefully consider the fees charged by different exchanges before engaging in arbitrage to ensure that they are able to make a profit.

Another important factor to consider when engaging in arbitrage in cryptocurrency markets is the liquidity of the cryptocurrencies being traded. Some cryptocurrencies have higher trading volumes and are more liquid than others, making it easier to buy and sell them quickly. Traders should consider the liquidity of the cryptocurrencies they are trading to ensure that they are able to execute trades quickly and efficiently.

Arbitrage in cryptocurrency markets can be a complex strategy that requires careful planning and execution. Traders should carefully research the market and understand how prices are determined on different exchangesbefore engaging in arbitrage. It is also important to have a solid understanding of the risks involved in arbitrage and to have a clear exit strategy in case prices move against you.

Overall, arbitrage in cryptocurrency markets can be a profitable trading strategy for those who understand how it works and are able to execute trades quickly and efficiently. By carefully considering factors such as fees, liquidity, and market conditions, traders can take advantage of price differences in the market and make a profitthrough arbitrage.

Arbitrage in cryptocurrency markets is a trading strategy that involves taking advantage of price differences between different exchanges or markets. It can be a profitable opportunity for those who understand how it works and are able to execute trades quickly and efficiently.

Traders should carefully consider factors such as fees, liquidity, and market conditions before engaging in arbitrage to ensure that they are able to make a profit. Arbitrage in cryptocurrency markets can be a risky strategy, but for those who are willing to take the risk,it can be a lucrative opportunity to profit from the inefficiencies in the market.

Implementing Arbitrage Strategies with Python scripts

Arbitrage is a trading strategy that involves taking advantage of price differences in different markets to make a profit. In the world of finance, arbitrage opportunities arise when the price of an asset is different in two or more markets. Traders can buy the asset in the market where it is cheaper and sell it in the market where it is more expensive to make a profit.

Implementing arbitrage strategies can be complex and time-consuming, but with the right tools and knowledge, it can be a lucrative way to make money in the financial markets. One popular tool for implementing arbitrage strategies is Python, a powerful programming language that is widely used in quantitative finance.

In this article, we will discuss how to implement arbitrage strategies using Python scripts. We will walk through a simple example of a triangular arbitrage strategy and provide step-by-step instructions on how to code it in Python.

Triangular arbitrage is a type of arbitrage strategy that involves trading three different currencies to take advantage of price discrepancies in the foreign exchange market. The basic idea behind triangular arbitrage is to find three currency pairs where the exchange rates do not match up, creating an opportunity for profit.

To implement a triangular arbitrage strategy in Python,

we will need to use a few key libraries: pandas, numpy, and ccxt. Pandas is a powerful data manipulation library that will help us work with the currency exchange rates, while numpy is a library for numerical computing that will help us perform calculations. CCXT is a cryptocurrency trading library that will allow us to access real-time exchange rate data from various cryptocurrency exchanges.

To get started, we will first need to install the necessary libraries. You can install pandas, numpy, and ccxt using the following commands:

```
```
pip install pandaspip install numpypip install ccxt
```
```

Once you have installed the libraries, you can start coding your triangular arbitrage strategy. Here is an example Python script that demonstrates how to implement a simple triangular arbitrage strategy:

```python
import pandas as pdimport numpy as npimport ccxt

# Initialize the exchange exchange = ccxt.binance()

# Get the exchange rate data exchange_data = exchange.fetch_tickers()
```

```python
# Create a DataFrame to store the exchange rate datadf =
pd.DataFrame(exchange_data)

# Filter the DataFrame to include only the currency pairs
we     are     interested     in     df     =
df[df['symbol'].str.contains('BTC/ETH|ETH/USDT|BTC/
USDT')]

# Calculate the arbitrage opportunity
df['arbitrage'] = (1 / df[df['symbol'] == 'BTC/ETH']['last'])
* df[df['symbol'] == 'ETH/USDT']['last'] * df[df['symbol']
== 'BTC/USDT']['last'] - 1

# Print the arbitrage opportunityprint(df)
```

In this script, we first import the necessary libraries and initialize the Binance exchange using the ccxt library. We then fetch the ticker data from the exchange and create a DataFrame to store the data. Next, we filter the DataFrame to include only the currency pairs we are interested in (BTC/ETH, ETH/USDT, and BTC/USDT). Finally, we calculate the arbitrage opportunity by multiplying the exchange rates for the three currency pairs and subtracting 1. The resulting DataFrame will show the arbitrage opportunity for each currency pair.

This is just a simple example of a triangular arbitrage strategy implemented in Python. There are many other arbitrage strategies that you can implement using Python, depending on your trading goals and risk tolerance. By leveraging the power of Python and the ccxt library, you can access real-time exchange rate data and quickly analyze arbitrage opportunities in the financial markets.

Implementing arbitrage strategies with Python scripts can be a profitable way to make money in the financial markets. By using the right tools and libraries, such as pandas, numpy, and ccxt, you can easily access exchange rate data and analyze arbitrage opportunities in real-time.

If you are interested in exploring arbitrage trading further, consider experimenting with different strategies and tweaking your Python scripts tooptimize your trading results. Happy trading!

Chapter 15: Advanced Trading Bot Development

In this chapter, we will delve into the world of advanced trading bot development. Building on the foundation laid in the previous chapters, we will explore more sophisticated strategies, techniques, and tools that can be used to create highly effective trading bots.

One of the key aspects of advanced trading bot development is the use of machine learning algorithms. Machine learning is a branch of artificial intelligence that enables computers to learn from and make predictions or decisions based on data. By incorporating machine learning algorithms into trading bots, developers can create bots that can adapt and evolve over time, making more accurate and profitable trades.

There are several types of machine learning algorithms that can be used in trading bots, including supervised learning, unsupervised learning, and reinforcement learning. Supervised learning involves training the bot on a labeled dataset, where the correct outcomes are known. Unsupervised learning involves training the bot on an unlabeled dataset, where the outcomes are unknown. Reinforcement learning involves training the bot through trial and error, where it learns from its mistakes and successes.

Another important aspect of advanced trading bot development is the use of advanced technical indicators.

Technical indicators are mathematical calculations based on the price, volume, or open interest of a security or market. These indicators can help traders identify trends, patterns, and potential trading opportunities. By incorporating advanced technical indicators into trading bots, developers can create bots that can make more informed and strategic trading decisions.

Some examples of advanced technical indicators that can be used in trading bots include moving averages, relative strength index (RSI), stochastic oscillator, and Bollinger Bands. These indicators can help traders identify overbought or oversold conditions, trend reversals, and potential entry and exit points.

In addition to machine learning algorithms and technical indicators, advanced trading bot development also involves the use of advanced risk management techniques. Risk management is a crucial aspect of trading, as it helps traders protect their capital and minimize losses. By incorporating advanced risk management technique into trading bots, developers can create bots that can effectively manage risk and maximize returns.

Some advanced risk management techniques that can be used in trading bots include position sizing, stop-loss orders, and diversification. Position sizing involves determining the amount of capital to allocate to each trade based on the risk of the trade. Stop-loss orders are orders placed to automatically sell a security when it reaches a certain price, thereby limiting potential losses. Diversification involves spreading capital across multiple trades or assets to reduce risk.

Overall, advanced trading bot development requires a deep understanding of machine learning algorithms, technical indicators, and risk management techniques. By incorporating these advanced strategies, techniques, and tools into trading bots, developers can create bots that are highly effective, adaptive, and profitable. As the field of algorithmic trading continues to evolve, advanced trading bot development will play an increasingly important role in the financial markets.

Enhancing Your Trading Bot

Trading bots have become increasingly popular in the world of finance and investing. These automated programs are designed to execute trades on behalf of the user, based on pre-defined parameters and strategies. While trading bots can be a powerful tool for investors, they are not without their limitations. In order to maximize the effectiveness of your trading bot, it is important to continuously enhance and optimize its performance.

There are several ways in which you can enhance your trading bot to improve its efficiency and profitability. In this article, we will explore some of the key strategies that you can implement to take your trading bot to the next level.

Backtesting

One of the most important steps in enhancing your trading bot is to conduct thorough backtesting. Backtesting involves running historical data through your trading bot to see how it would have performed in the past. This allows you to identify any weaknesses or inefficiencies in your bot's strategy and make adjustments accordingly.

By backtesting your trading bot, you can gain valuable insights into its performance and identify areas for improvement. You can also test different strategies and parameters to see which ones are most effective in different market conditions. This will help you to refine your bot's trading strategy and increase its profitability over time.

Optimize your trading strategy

Once you have conducted thorough backtesting, it is important to optimize your trading strategy based on the results. This may involve tweaking your bot's parameters, adjusting its risk management settings, or implementing new trading indicators. By continuously refining your trading strategy, you can improve your bot's performance and increase its profitability.

It is important to remember that the markets are constantly changing, and what works today may not work tomorrow. By staying up-to-date with market trends and adjusting your trading strategy accordingly, you can ensure that your bot remains competitive and profitable in the long run.

Implement risk management protocols

Risk management is a critical component of successful trading bot operation. Without proper risk management protocols in place, your bot may be exposed to unnecessary risks and potential losses. It is important to implement strict risk management rules, such as setting stop-loss orders, position sizing limits, and maximum drawdown thresholds.

By implementing effective risk management protocols, you can protect your trading capital and minimize the impact of potential losses. This will help to ensure the long-term viability of your trading bot and increase its overall profitability.

Diversify your trading strategy

Another way to enhance your trading bot is to diversify its trading strategy. Instead of relying on a single strategy or asset class, consider incorporating multiple strategies and trading instruments into your bot's portfolio. This will help to spread risk and increase the potential for profit.

Diversification can also help to reduce the impact of market volatility and unexpected events. By trading across different markets and asset classes, you can hedge against potential losses and increase the overall stability of your bot's performance.

Monitor and analyze performance

In order to enhance your trading bot, it is important to regularly monitor and analyze its performance. Keep track of key metrics such as win rate, profitability, drawdown, and trading volume. By analyzing these metrics, you can identify patterns and trends in your bot's performance and make informed decisions about how to optimize its operation.

It is also important to keep an eye on market conditions and adjust your trading strategy accordingly. By staying informed about market trends and news events, you can make timely adjustments to your bot's strategy and maximize its profitability.

Utilize advanced trading tools and technologies

To enhance your trading bot, consider utilizing advanced trading tools and technologies. These tools can help to automate various aspects of your trading strategy, such as technical analysis, risk management, and trade execution. By leveraging these tools, you can increase the efficiency and effectiveness of your bot's operation.

Some advanced trading tools to consider include algorithmic trading platforms, trading signal services, and data analytics software. These tools can help you to identify profitable trading opportunities, optimize your trading strategy, and improve your bot's overall performance.

Stay informed and adapt to market changes

Finally, in order to enhance your trading bot, it is important to stay informed about market changes and adapt accordingly. The financial markets are constantly evolving, and what works today may not work tomorrow. By staying up-to-date with market trends, news events, and economic indicators, you can make informed decisions about how to optimize your bot's trading strategy.

It is also important to be flexible and willing to adapt to changing market conditions. By adjusting your trading strategy in response to market changes, you can ensure that your bot remains competitive and profitable over the long term.

Enhancing your trading bot is a continuous process that

requires careful analysis, optimization, and adaptation. By implementing the strategies outlined in this article, you can improve the efficiency and profitability of your trading bot and achieve greater success in the financial markets.

By backtesting your bot, optimizing your trading strategy, implementing risk management protocols, diversifying your trading strategy, monitoring and analyzing performance,

Using AI and ML to Improve Bot Performance with python - scripts

Artificial Intelligence (AI) and Machine Learning (ML) have become integral parts of modern technology, revolutionizing the way we interact with machines and systems. One area where AI and ML have made significant advancements is in the development of chatbots. Chatbots are computer programs that simulate human conversation through text or voice interactions. They are used in a wide range of applications, from customer service to online shopping.

Python is a popular programming language for developing chatbots due to its simplicity and versatility. In this article, we will explore how AI and ML can be used to improve bot performance in Python, with examples of scripts that demonstrate these concepts.

Improving Bot Performance with AI and ML

AI and ML technologies can enhance chatbot performance in several ways. These technologies enable chatbots to understand and respond to user queries more accurately and efficiently. By analyzing large amounts of data, AI and ML algorithms can help chatbots learn from past interactions and improve their responses over time.

Here are some ways in which AI and ML can be used to enhance chatbot performance:

Natural Language Processing (NLP): NLP is a branch of

AI that focuses on the interaction between computers and human language. NLP algorithms enable chatbots to understand and interpret user queries in a more natural way. By using NLP, chatbots can analyze the context of a conversation and provide more relevant responses.

Sentiment Analysis: Sentiment analysis is a technique used to determine the emotional tone of a text. By analyzing user messages, chatbots can gauge the sentiment of a conversation and tailor their responses accordingly. This can help chatbots provide more personalized and empathetic interactions with users.

Machine Learning Models: Machine learning algorithms can be used to train chatbots on large datasets of conversations. By analyzing these datasets, chatbots can learn patterns in user behavior and improve their responses over time. Machine learning models can also be used to predict user intent and suggest appropriate responses.

Reinforcement Learning: Reinforcement learning is a type of machine learning that enables chatbots to learn through trial and error. By rewarding chatbots for correct responses and penalizing them for incorrect ones, reinforcement learning algorithms can help chatbots improve their performance through continuous feedback.

Python Scripts Example

Now, let's take a look at some Python scripts that demonstrate how AI and ML can be used to improve chatbot performance:

Natural Language Processing (NLP) with NLTK: import nltk

```
from nltk.tokenize import word_tokenize
# Sample user query
user_query = "What is the weather like today?"

# Tokenize user query
tokens = word_tokenize(user_query)

# Part-of-speech tagging pos_tags  = nltk.pos_tag(tokens)

print(pos_tags)
```

In this script, we use the NLTK library to perform natural language processing on a user query. We tokenize the user query and then perform part-of-speech tagging to identify the grammatical structure of the sentence.

Sentiment Analysis with TextBlob:

```
from textblob import TextBlob# Sample user message
user_message = "I love this product! It's amazing."

# Perform sentiment analysis
sentiment         =         TextBlob(user_message).sentiment
print(sentiment)
```

In this script, we use the TextBlob library to perform sentiment analysis on a user message. We analyze the emotional tone of the message and determine whether it is positive, negative, or neutral.

Machine Learning Model with Scikit-Learn:

```
from        sklearn.feature_extraction.text        import
```

CountVectorizer from sklearn.naive_bayes import MultinomialNB

```
# Sample dataset
X_train = ["Hello, how can I help you?", "What is your name?", "Tell me a joke."] y_train = ["greeting", "question", "humor"]

# Vectorize text data vectorizer = CountVectorizer()
X_train_counts = vectorizer.fit_transform(X_train)

# Train a Naive Bayes classifier clf = MultinomialNB()
clf.fit(X_train_counts, y_train)


# Sample user query user_query = "What time is it?"

# Vectorize user query
X_test = vectorizer.transform([user_query])

# Predict intent
predicted_intent           =           clf.predict(X_test)
print(predicted_intent)
```
In this script, we use the Scikit-Learn library to train a machine learning model on a dataset of user queries and their corresponding intents. We vectorize the text data using a Count Vectorizer and then train a Naive Bayes classifier to predict the intent of a user query.

We have explored how AI and ML can be used to improve chatbot performance in Python. By leveraging these technologies, chatbots can provide more accurate and personalized interactions with users. With the help of NLP, sentiment analysis, machine learning models, and reinforcement learning, chatbots can continuously learn and improve their responses over time.

Chapter 16: High-Frequency Trading (HFT) in Cryptocurrencies

High-frequency trading (HFT) is a form of trading that uses powerful computers to execute a large number of orders at extremely high speeds. This type of trading is prevalent in traditional financial markets, but it has also made its way into the world of cryptocurrencies. In this chapter, we will explore the impact of HFT on the cryptocurrency market and how it has changed the landscape of trading in digital assets.

HFT in cryptocurrencies operates in a similar manner to traditional markets, with traders using sophisticated algorithms to analyze market data and execute trades within microseconds. These algorithms are designed to exploit small price differentials and market inefficiencies, allowing HFT traders to profit from rapid changes in prices. The use of HFT in cryptocurrencies has grown significantly in recent years, as the market has become more liquid and volatile.

One of the key advantages of HFT in cryptocurrencies is its ability to provide liquidity to the market. By constantly placing and canceling orders, HFT traders help to ensure that there is always a buyer or seller available for a particular asset. This can help to reduce price volatility and improve market efficiency, making it easier for other traders to execute their trades at fair prices.

However, HFT in cryptocurrencies has also been criticized

for exacerbating market volatility and creating unfair advantages for high-frequency traders. Critics argue that HFT can lead to rapid price swings and market manipulation, as traders with faster access to market data and execution speeds can exploit slower market participants. This can create a two-tiered market, where HFT traders have an unfair advantage over retail traders and institutional investors.

Another concern with HFT in cryptocurrencies is the potential for market abuse and manipulation. Because HFT traders can execute trades at such high speeds, there is a risk that they could engage in illegal activities such as front-running or spoofing. Front-running involves placing orders based on non-public information, while spoofing involves placing fake orders to manipulate prices. These practices can distort market prices and harm other market participants, leading to regulatory scrutiny and potential legal action.

Despite these concerns, HFT in cryptocurrencies continues to grow in popularity, as traders seek to capitalize on the fast-paced nature of the market. Many exchanges now offer co-location services, which allow HFT traders to place their servers in close proximity to the exchange's matching engine, reducing latency and improving execution speeds. This has led to a proliferation of HFT firms in the cryptocurrency space, with some estimates suggesting that they account for a significant portion of daily trading volume.

In conclusion, HFT has had a significant impact on the cryptocurrency market, bringing both benefits and challenges. While it can provide liquidity and improve market efficiency, it also raises concerns about market manipulation and unfair advantages for high-frequency traders. As the cryptocurrency market continues to evolve, regulators will need to carefully monitor the activities of HFT firms and ensure that they are operating in a fair and transparent manner. Only then can the market reach its full potential as a reliable and efficient trading platform for digital assets.

Introduction to Frequency Trading HFT

One of the key advantages of HFT is its speed. By using high-speed computers and sophisticated algorithms, HFT firms are able to execute trades in fractions of a second, allowing them to take advantage of even the smallest price differentials. This speed gives HFT firms a significant edge over traditional traders, who may take much longer to enter and exit positions.

Another advantage of HFT is its ability to generate large volumes of trades. HFT firms can execute thousands of trades in a single day, which can lead to significant profits over time. By taking advantage of small price discrepancies and executing a large number of trades, HFT firms can generate consistent returns, even in volatile market conditions.

However, HFT is not without its risks. The speed and volume of trades executed by HFT firms can sometimes exacerbate market volatility, leading to sudden and unpredictable price movements. Additionally, the reliance on complex algorithms and high-speed technology can make HFT vulnerable to technical glitches and system failures, which can result in significant losses.

Despite these risks, HFT continues to be a popular trading strategy among institutional investors and hedge funds. The potential for high returns and the ability to capitalize on market inefficiencies make HFT an attractive option for those looking to maximize their trading profits.

In recent years, there has been increasing scrutiny of HFT by regulators and policymakers. Concerns have been raised about the impact of HFT on market stability and fairness, as well as the potential for market manipulation. Regulators have implemented measures to address these concerns, such as imposing stricter regulations on HFT firms and increasing oversight of the industry.

Overall, HFT is a complex and controversial trading strategy that has the potential to generate significant profits for those who are able to master it. While the speed and volume of trades executed by HFT firms can lead to increased market volatility and potential risks, the ability to capitalize on small price discrepancies can also result in substantial returns. As technology continues to advance and markets become increasingly interconnected, HFT is likely to remain a prominent feature of the financial landscape for years to come.

Implementing HFT Strategies with Python scripts

High-frequency trading (HFT) is a type of algorithmic trading that involves the use of powerful computers to execute trades at incredibly high speeds. HFT strategies are designed to capitalize on small price movements in the market, often taking advantage of inefficiencies or discrepancies in pricing. Implementing HFT strategies can be complex and challenging, but with the right tools and knowledge, it is possible to achieve success in this fast-paced and competitive environment.

One popular programming language for implementing HFT strategies is Python. Python is a versatile and powerful language that is widely used in the financial industry for data analysis, algorithmic trading, and quantitative modeling. In this article, we will explore how Python can be used to implement HFT strategies, and provide an example of a simple HFT strategy using Python scripts.

To implement HFT strategies with Python, you will need to have a good understanding of the language, as well as knowledge of finance and trading concepts. You will also need access to real-time market data, either through a data provider or an API. Python libraries such as pandas, numpy, and matplotlib can be used for data analysis and visualization, while libraries such as requests and websocket-client can be used for connecting to market data feeds.

One important consideration when implementing HFT

strategies is latency. Latency refers to the time it takes for a trade to be executed after an order is placed, and in the world of HFT, milliseconds can make a significant difference in profitability. To minimize latency, it is important to optimize your code for speed and efficiency, and to use high-performance hardware and network connections.

Now, let's look at an example of a simple HFT strategy using Python scripts. In this example, we will implement a mean reversion strategy, which involves buying a security when its price is below its historical average, and selling it when its price is above its historical average.

First, we will import the necessary libraries:

```python
import numpy as np import pandas as pd
import matplotlib.pyplot as plt import requests
import time
```

Next, we will define a function to fetch historical price data for a given security:

```python
def fetch_data(symbol, start_date, end_date):
    url = f'https://api.marketdataapi.com/v1/ohlcv/{symbol}?start={start_date}&end={end_date}'    response = requests.get(url)
    data = response.json()
    df = pd.DataFrame(data['data'], columns=['timestamp',
```

'open', 'high', 'low', 'close', 'volume']) df['timestamp'] = pd.to_datetime(df['timestamp'], unit='s')

df.set_index('timestamp', inplace=True)return df
```

Now, we will define a function to calculate the historical average price for a given security:

```python
def calculate_average_price(df, window):
df['average_price']                                    =
df['close'].rolling(window=window).mean()return df
```

Next, we will define a function to implement the mean reversion strategy:

```python
def mean_reversion_strategy(df, window, threshold):
df['position'] = np.where(df['close'] < df['average_price'] -
threshold, 1, 0) df['position'] = np.where(df['close'] >
df['average_price'] + threshold, -1, df['position'])return df
```

Finally, we will define a function to backtest the strategy and visualize the results:

```python
def backtest_strategy(df, window, threshold):
df = calculate_average_price(df, window)
df = mean_reversion_strategy(df, window, threshold)
df['returns']             =             df['position'].shift(1)        *
```
```

```
df['close'].pct_change() df['cumulative_returns'] = (1 +
df['returns']).cumprod() df['cumulative_returns'].plot()
plt.show()
```

To run the strategy, we will first fetch historical price data
for a security:

```python
symbol = 'AAPL' start_date = '2022-01-01'
end_date = '2022-02-01'
df = fetch_data(symbol, start_date, end_date)
```

Next, we will backtest the strategy with a 30-day moving
average window and a threshold of 0.1:

```python window = 30
threshold = 0.1
```

```
backtest_strategy(df, window, threshold)
```

By running this code, we can visualize the performance of the mean reversion strategy on historical price data for a given security. This is just a simple example of an HFT strategy implemented with Python scripts, and there are many more advanced strategies that can be developed using Python and other programming languages.

Chapter 17: Regulations and Compliance in Cryptocurrency Trading

In recent years, the cryptocurrency market has experienced tremendous growth, attracting millions of investors and traders from around the world. However, with this rapid expansion comes increased scrutiny from regulators and policymakers who are seeking to establish rules and guidelines to ensure the safety and security of participants in the market. In this chapter, we will explore the various regulations and compliance requirements that govern cryptocurrency trading and the implications they have for traders and investors.

Regulation of cryptocurrency trading varies significantly from country to country, with some jurisdictions embracing the new technology and others taking a more cautious approach. In the United States, for example, the Securities and Exchange Commission (SEC) has taken a proactive stance on regulating cryptocurrency trading, issuing guidelines and warnings to investors about the risks involved in trading digital assets. The Commodity Futures Trading Commission (CFTC) also plays a role in regulating cryptocurrency derivatives, such as futures and options.

In Europe, the European Securities and Markets Authority (ESMA) has issued guidelines on the regulation of cryptocurrencies, urging member states to adopt a common approach to regulating digital assets. In Asia, countries like Japan and South Korea have taken a more permissive approach to regulating cryptocurrency trading, with Japan even going so far as to legalize Bitcoin as a form of payment.

One of the key challenges facing regulators in the cryptocurrency market is the decentralized nature of the technology. Unlike traditional financial markets, where regulators can monitor and enforce compliance through centralized exchanges, cryptocurrencies are traded on a network of decentralized exchanges and peer-to-peer platforms, making it difficult for regulators to track and regulate transactions.

To address this challenge, regulators have focused on implementing know-your-customer (KYC) and anti-money laundering (AML) regulations on cryptocurrency exchanges and trading platforms. These regulations require exchanges to verify the identity of their users and report suspicious transactions to authorities, in an effort to prevent money laundering and other illicit activities.

In addition to KYC and AML regulations, regulators have also taken steps to protect investors from fraud and market manipulation in the cryptocurrency market. The SEC, for example, has cracked down on fraudulent initial coin offerings (ICOs) and Ponzi schemes, issuing cease-and-desist orders and fines to companies that violate securities laws.

Another area of concern for regulators is the volatility and lack of transparency in the cryptocurrency market. Unlike traditional financial markets, where trading is conducted on regulated exchanges with clear rules and oversight, cryptocurrency trading is often conducted on unregulated platforms with little transparency or accountability.

To address these concerns, regulators have proposed a range of measures to increase transparency and stability in the cryptocurrency market. Some regulators have called for the establishment of a global regulatory framework for cryptocurrencies, while others have proposed stricter oversight of exchanges and trading platforms.

Despite these challenges, the cryptocurrency market continues to attract a growing number of investors and traders, drawn by the potential for high returns and the promise of a decentralized financial system. As the market matures, regulators will continue to play a crucial role in shaping its development and ensuring the safety and security of participants.

Regulations and compliance are essential aspects of cryptocurrency trading that can help protect investors and ensure the stability of the market. By adhering to regulatory guidelines and best practices, traders and investors can help promote a more transparent and secure trading environment for all participants.

As the cryptocurrency market continues to evolve, it is important for regulators and policymakers to work together with industry stakeholders to develop a balanced and effective regulatory framework that supports innovation while safeguarding the interests of investors.

Understanding Regulatory Challenges in Cryptocurrency Trading

The rise of cryptocurrency trading has brought about a new wave of financial innovation, with digital assets such as Bitcoin, Ethereum, and others gaining popularity as alternative investment options. However, along with this growth comes a host of regulatory challenges that both traders and regulators must navigate to ensure the integrity and stability of the market.

One of the major challenges facing regulators in the cryptocurrency trading space is the lack of a uniform regulatory framework. Unlike traditional financial markets, which are governed by established regulatory bodies such as the Securities and Exchange Commission (SEC) in the United States, the cryptocurrency market operates across international borders and is subject to a patchwork of regulations that vary from country to country.

This lack of uniformity can create confusion for traders and make it difficult for regulators to effectively monitor and enforce compliance with existing laws. In some cases, regulatory uncertainty can even deter investors from participating in the market, leading to decreased liquidity and increased volatility.

Another challenge facing regulators in the cryptocurrency trading space is the prevalence of fraudulent and illegal activities. The decentralized nature of the blockchain technology that underpins most cryptocurrencies makes it difficult for regulators to track and trace illicit transactions, such as money laundering, terrorist financing, and other criminal activities.

In response to these challenges, regulators around the world have taken steps to tighten oversight of the cryptocurrency market. In the United States, for example, the SEC has issued guidelines for initial coin offerings (ICOs) and other cryptocurrency-related activities, while the Commodity Futures Trading Commission (CFTC) has classified Bitcoin and other cryptocurrencies as commodities subject to its jurisdiction.

Similarly, in Europe, the European Securities and Markets Authority (ESMA) has called for a coordinated approach to regulating cryptocurrencies, while individual countries such as Germany and France have proposed their own regulations to govern the market.

Despite these efforts, however, regulatory challenges in the cryptocurrency trading space persist. One of the key issues facing regulators is the difficulty of enforcing compliance with existing laws, particularly in cases where transactions occur across international borders or involve anonymous parties.

In addition, the rapid pace of technological innovation in the cryptocurrency space means that regulations can quickly become outdated or ineffective, requiring regulators to constantly adapt and evolve their oversight mechanisms to keep pace with changing market dynamics.

Another challenge facing regulators is the potential for regulatory arbitrage, where traders seek out jurisdictions with lax regulations or enforcement mechanisms to conduct illicit activities. This can create a race to the bottom in terms of regulatory standards, undermining efforts to promote transparency and accountability in the market.

To address these challenges, regulators must work together to develop a coordinated approach to regulating the cryptocurrency trading space. This may involve harmonizing existing regulations, sharing information and bestpractices, and collaborating on enforcement actions to crack down on fraudulent and illegal activities.

In addition, regulators should work closely with industry stakeholders, such as cryptocurrency exchanges, wallet providers, and other service providers, to develop industry best practices and standards that promote transparency, security, and compliance with existing regulations.

Finally, regulators must also invest in developing the technological capabilities and expertise needed to effectively monitor and enforce compliance with existing laws in the cryptocurrency trading space. This may involve deploying advanced data analytics tools, blockchain analysis software, and other technologies to track and trace illicit transactions and identify suspicious activities.

Overall, while regulatory challenges in the cryptocurrency trading space are significant, they are not insurmountable. By working together and adopting a proactive and collaborative approach to regulation, regulators can help ensure the integrity and stability of the market while promoting innovation and growth in the digital asset space.

Staying Compliant in the Cryptocurrency Market

The cryptocurrency market has seen tremendous growth in recent years, with more and more individuals and institutions getting involved in trading and investing in digital assets. However, with this growth comes increased scrutiny from regulators and government agencies, which means that staying compliant in the cryptocurrency market is more important than ever.

One of the key challenges in staying compliant in the cryptocurrency market is the lack of clear regulations and guidelines from governments and regulatory bodies. While some countries have taken steps to regulate the cryptocurrency market, many others have yet to do so, leaving investors and traders in a state of uncertainty.

However, despite the lack of clear regulations, there are still steps that individuals and institutions can take to stay compliant in the cryptocurrency market. One of the most important things to do is to ensure that you are following all relevant laws and regulations in your jurisdiction. This means understanding the tax implications of trading and investing in cryptocurrencies, as well as any reporting requirements that may apply to you.

Another important step in staying compliant in the cryptocurrency market is to be aware of the risks associated with trading and investing in digital assets. Cryptocurrencies are highly volatile and can be subject to manipulation and fraud, so it is important to do your due diligence before getting involved in the market. This includes researching the projects and teams behind the cryptocurrencies you are interested in, as well as understanding the technology and security measures that are in place to protect your investments.

In addition to understanding the risks associated with trading and investing in cryptocurrencies, it is also important to be aware of the potential for money laundering and other illegal activities in the cryptocurrency market. Because cryptocurrencies are decentralized and can be traded anonymously, they have been used by criminals to launder money and finance illegal activities. As a result, regulators and government agencies are increasingly cracking down on illicit activities in the cryptocurrency market, and individuals and institutions that are found to be involved in such activities can face severe penalties.

To stay compliant in the cryptocurrency market, it is important to implement strong Know Your Customer (KYC) and Anti-Money Laundering (AML) procedures. This means verifying the identities of your customers and conducting due diligence on their transactions to ensure that they are not involved in any illegal activities. By implementing robust KYC and AML procedures, you can protect yourself and your business from potential legal and regulatory risks.

Another important aspect of staying compliant in the cryptocurrency market is to keep detailed records of all your transactions and activities. This includes keeping records of your trades, investments, and any communications you have with customers or counterparties. By maintaining accurate and up-to-date records, you can demonstrate to regulators and government agencies that you are operating in a transparent and compliant manner.

In addition to keeping detailed records, it is also important to stay informed about developments in the cryptocurrency market and any changes to regulations or guidelines that may affect your business. This means staying up-to-date on the latest news and trends in the cryptocurrency market, as well as attending conferences and events where you can network with other industry professionals and learn from experts in the field.

Finally, to stay compliant in the cryptocurrency market, it is important to work with reputable partners and service providers. This includes choosing exchanges and wallets that have strong security measures in place to protect your assets, as well as working with legal and compliance experts who can help you navigate the complex regulatory landscape of the cryptocurrency market.

Staying compliant in the cryptocurrency market is essential for individuals and institutions who want to operate in a legal and transparent manner. By following the steps outlined in this article, you can protect yourself and your business from potential legal and regulatory risks, and ensure that you are operating in a compliant and ethical manner. Remember to always do your due diligence, keep accurate records, and work with reputable partners to stay compliant in the cryptocurrency market.

Chapter 18: Security and Privacy in Cryptocurrency Trading

In recent years, the popularity of cryptocurrency trading has surged, with more and more people investing in digital currencies like Bitcoin, Ethereum, and Litecoin. However, with the rise in popularity of cryptocurrency trading, there has also been a corresponding increase in security and privacy concerns. In this chapter, we will explore the importance of security and privacy in cryptocurrency trading and discuss some best practices for keeping your investments safe.

Security in cryptocurrency trading is of utmost importance, as the decentralized and digital nature of cryptocurrencies makes them vulnerable to hacking and theft. Unlike traditional financial systems, where banks and other financial institutions provide security measures to protect your funds, in the world of cryptocurrencies, you are responsible for safeguarding your own assets.

One of the most important security measures in cryptocurrency trading is the use of secure wallets. Cryptocurrency wallets are digital tools that allow you to store, send, and receive digital currencies. There are different types of wallets available, including hardware wallets, software wallets, and paper wallets. Hardware wallets are considered the most secure option, as they store your private keys offline, making them less vulnerable to hacking attacks.

Another important security measure in cryptocurrency trading is the use of two-factor authentication (2FA). 2FA adds an extra layer of security to your accounts by requiring you to provide two pieces of information to log in, such as a password and a unique code sent to your phone. This helps protect your accounts from unauthorized access, even if your password is compromised.

In addition to using secure wallets and 2FA, it is also important to be cautious when trading cryptocurrencies online. Be wary of phishing scams, where malicious actors try to trick you into revealing your private keys or other sensitive information. Only trade on reputable exchanges and avoid clicking on suspicious links or downloading unknown software.

Privacy is another important aspect of cryptocurrency trading. While the blockchain technology that underpins cryptocurrencies is designed to be transparent and secure, it is also important to protect your privacy when trading digital currencies. One way to do this is by using privacy coins, such as Monero or Zcash, which offer enhanced privacy features like stealth addresses and ring signatures.

It is also important to be mindful of the information you share online when trading cryptocurrencies. Avoid using your real name or other identifying information on public forums or social media platforms, as this can make you a target for hackers and scammers. Keep your trading activities private and only share information with trusted individuals.

In conclusion, security and privacy are paramount in cryptocurrency trading. By using secure wallets, implementing 2FA, and being cautious online, you can protect your investments from hacking and theft. Additionally, by using privacy coins and being mindful of the information you share online, you can safeguard your privacy while trading digital currencies. Remember to always stay informed and be proactive in protecting your assets in the fast-paced world of cryptocurrency trading.

Securing Your Trading Environment with python - scripts

In today's fast-paced trading environment, it is crucial to ensure that your systems are secure and protected from potential threats. One way to enhance the security of your trading environment is by using Python scripts to automate security measures and monitor your systems for any suspicious activity.

Python is a versatile programming language that is widely used for automation, data analysis, and web development. It is also a popular choice for creating security scripts due to its simplicity and readability. In this article, we will explore how Python scripts can be used to secure your trading environment and protect your sensitive data.

One of the first steps in securing your trading environment with Python is to ensure that your systems are up todate with the latest security patches and updates. Python scripts can be used to automate the process of checkingfor updates and applying them to your systems. By regularly updating your software, you can protect your systems from known vulnerabilities and reduce the risk of a security breach.

Another important aspect of securing your trading environment is monitoring your systems for any unusual activity. Python scripts can be used to create custom monitoring tools that alert you to any suspicious behavior, such as unauthorized login attempts or unusual network traffic. By monitoring your systems in real-time, you can quickly identify and respond to potential security threats before they escalate.

In addition to monitoring your systems, Python scripts can also be used to implement access controls and encryption to protect your sensitive data. For example, you can use Python scripts to enforce strong password policies, restrict access to certain files or directories, and encrypt data both at rest and in transit. By implementing these security measures, you can reduce the risk of unauthorized access to your trading environment and protect your valuable assets.

Furthermore, Python scripts can be used to automate the process of backing up your data and creating disaster recovery plans. By regularly backing up your data to secure locations, you can ensure that you can quickly recover from any data loss or system failure. Python scripts can also be used to test your disaster recovery plans and simulate different scenarios to ensure that your systems are resilient to potential threats.

Another important aspect of securing your trading environment with Python is to implement strong authentication mechanisms. Python scripts can be used to create multi-factor authentication systems that require users to provide multiple forms of identification, such as a password and a one-time code sent to their mobile device. By implementing multi-factor authentication, you can significantly reduce the risk of unauthorized access to your systems and protect your sensitive data.

In addition to securing your trading environment, Python

scripts can also be used to analyze and visualize your trading data to identify patterns and trends. By using Python libraries such as Pandas and Matplotlib, you can create custom dashboards and reports that provide insights into your trading activities and help you make informed decisions. By analyzing your trading data, you can identify potential risks and opportunities and optimize your trading strategies accordingly.

Overall, securing your trading environment with Python scripts is essential to protect your sensitive data and ensure the integrity of your systems. By automating security measures, monitoring your systems for suspicious activity, implementing access controls and encryption, and analyzing your trading data, you can enhance the security of your trading environment and reduce the risk of a security breach.

Python's versatility and simplicity make it an ideal choice for creating security scripts that can help you secure your trading environment effectively.

Protecting Your Digital Assets with python - scripts

Protecting your digital assets has become more important than ever. With the rise of cyber threats and data breaches, it is crucial to take steps to safeguard your sensitive information and prevent unauthorized access to your digital files. One way to enhance the security of your digital assets is by using Python scripts to automate tasks and implement security measures.

Python is a versatile programming language that is widely used for various applications, including cybersecurity. With its simplicity and flexibility, Python allows users to create powerful scripts that can help protect their digital assets from potential threats. In this article, we will explore how Python scripts can be used to enhance the security of your digital assets and provide examples of scripts that you can use to protect your data.

One of the key benefits of using Python scripts for cybersecurity is automation. By writing scripts to automate routine tasks, such as scanning for malware or monitoring network traffic, you can save time and ensure that your digital assets are constantly protected. For example, you can write a Python script that scans your computer for malicious files and alerts you if any suspicious activity is detected. This can help you identify and remove potential threats before they can cause harm to your digital assets.

Another advantage of using Python scripts for

cybersecurity is their flexibility. Python is a high-level programming language that is easy to learn and use, making it accessible to users with varying levels of technical expertise. Whether you are a beginner or an experienced programmer, you can write Python scripts to protect your digital assets effectively. Additionally, Python has a large community of developers who regularly contribute to open-source projects, providing a wealth of resources and support for users looking to enhance their cybersecurity practices.

To demonstrate how Python scripts can be used to protect your digital assets, let's consider a few examples of scripts that you can implement in your cybersecurity strategy:

File encryption script: One of the most effective ways to protect your digital assets is by encrypting sensitive files. You can write a Python script that encrypts your files using a secure encryption algorithm, such as AES. This script can prompt you for a password and then encrypt the selected files, making them unreadable to unauthorized users. By decrypting the files with the same password, you can ensure that only authorized individuals can access your sensitive information.

Network monitoring script: Monitoring network traffic is essential for detecting potential cyber threats and unauthorized access to your digital assets. You can write a Python script that captures network packets and analyzes them for suspicious activity, such as unusual data transfers or unauthorized connections. This script can alert you to any potential security breaches and help you take immediate action to protect your digital assets.

206

Password manager script: Managing passwords is a critical aspect of cybersecurity, as weak or reused passwords can make your digital assets vulnerable to attacks. You can write a Python script that generates strong, unique passwords for each of your accounts and stores them securely in an encrypted database. This script can also help you automatically fill in login forms and ensure that your passwords are not easily compromised.

Backup automation script: Regularly backing up your digital assets is essential for protecting them from dataloss due to hardware failure or cyber attacks. You can write a Python script that automates the backup process by copying your files to an external storage device or cloud storage service. This script can run on a scheduled basis to ensure that your data is always backed up and secure.

Intrusion detection script: Detecting intrusions and unauthorized access to your digital assets is crucial for maintaining cybersecurity. You can write a Python script that monitors system logs and network activity for signs of suspicious behavior, such as multiple failed login attempts or unusual file access. This script can alert you to potential security threats and help you take proactive measures to protect your digital assets.

Python scripts can be a valuable tool for protecting your digital assets and enhancing your cybersecurity practices. By automating tasks, implementing security measures, and monitoring for potential threats, you can ensure that your sensitive information remains secure and inaccessible to unauthorized users.

Whether you are a beginner or an experienced programmer, Python provides a user-friendly and effective platform for enhancing the security of your digital assets. By incorporating Python scripts into your cybersecurity strategy, you can take proactive steps to safeguard your digital files and protect them from potential cyber threats.

Chapter 19: Developing Custom Trading Indicators

In the world of trading, having the right tools and indicators can make all the difference between success and failure. While there are many pre-built indicators available for traders to use, developing custom trading indicators can give you a unique edge in the market. In this chapter, we will explore the process of developing custom trading indicators and how they can be used to improve your trading strategy.

Why Develop Custom Trading Indicators?

There are several reasons why traders may choose to develop custom trading indicators. One of the main advantages of custom indicators is that they can be tailored to fit a trader's specific needs and trading style. By developing custom indicators, traders can create tools that are unique to their trading strategy and provide them with a competitive advantage in the market.

Custom indicators can also help traders to better understand market trends and patterns. By developing indicators that are specifically designed to analyze certain aspects of the market, traders can gain deeper insights into market movements and make more informed trading decisions.

Additionally, custom indicators can be used to automate trading strategies. By developing indicators that generate buy and sell signals based on specific criteria, traders can create automated trading systems that execute trades without the need for manual intervention.

Overall, developing custom trading indicators can help traders to improve their trading strategy, gain a competitive edge in the market, and automate their trading process.

Steps to Develop Custom Trading Indicators

Developing custom trading indicators requires a combination of technical knowledge, programming skills, and an understanding of market dynamics. Here are some steps to help you develop custom trading indicators:

Define Your Trading Strategy: Before you start developing custom indicators, it is important to define your trading strategy. Consider what indicators would be most useful in helping you to identify trade opportunities, manage risk, and optimize your trading performance.

Choose a Programming Language: To develop custom trading indicators, you will need to choose a programming language that is compatible with your trading platform. Some popular programming languages for developing custom indicators include Python, C++, and MQL4.

Learn the Basics of Indicator Development: To develop custom trading indicators, you will need to learn the basics of indicator development, including how to calculate and plot data, create buy and sell signals, and test the effectiveness of your indicators.

Develop Your Indicator: Once you have a clear understanding of your trading strategy and the basics of indicator development, you can start developing your custom indicator. This may involve writing code to calculate specific data points, plot indicators on a chart, and generate buy and sell signals.

Test Your Indicator: After developing your custom indicator, it is important to test its effectiveness in a simulated trading environment. This will help you to identify any potential issues or limitations with your indicator and make any necessary adjustments.

Optimize Your Indicator: Once you have tested your custom indicator, you may need to optimize it to improve its performance. This may involve fine-tuning the parameters of your indicator, adjusting the calculation method, or incorporating additional data sources.

Implement Your Indicator: Once you are satisfied with the performance of your custom indicator, you can implement it into your trading platform and start using it in live trading.

Using Custom Trading Indicators

Once you have developed custom trading indicators, there are several ways you can use them to improve your trading strategy:

Identify Trade Opportunities: Custom indicators can help

you to identify potential trade opportunities by analyzing market trends, patterns, and price movements. By using custom indicators to generate buy and sell signals, you can make more informed trading decisions and improve your chances of success.

Manage Risk: Custom indicators can also help you to manage risk by providing you with insights into market volatility, trend strength, and potential price reversals. By incorporating risk management indicators into your trading strategy, you can minimize losses and protect your capital.

Automate Trading: Custom indicators can be used to automate trading strategies by generating buy and sell signals based on specific criteria. By developing automated trading systems that incorporate custom indicators, you can execute trades more efficiently and take advantage of market opportunities in real-time.

Optimize Performance: Custom indicators can be used to optimize the performance of your trading strategy by fine-tuning parameters, adjusting calculation methods, and incorporating additional data sources. By continuously monitoring and optimizing your custom indicators, you can improve your trading performance and stay ahead of the competition.

In conclusion, developing custom trading indicators can provide traders with a unique edge in the market by tailoring tools to fit their specific needs and trading style. By following the steps outlined in this chapter and using custom indicators effectively, traders can improve their trading strategy, gain a competitive advantage, and achieve greater success in the market.

Custom Indicators for Exchanges in Trading with python - scripts

Custom indicators play a crucial role in trading as they help traders analyze market trends and make informed decisions. In the world of cryptocurrency trading, custom indicators can be particularly useful as the market is highly volatile and constantly changing. One popular programming language used for creating custom indicators in trading is Python.

Python is a versatile and powerful programming language that is widely used in the world of finance and trading.Its simplicity and flexibility make it an ideal choice for creating custom indicators for exchanges. In this article, we will explore how to create custom indicators for exchanges in trading using Python scripts.

To create custom indicators for exchanges in trading, you will need to have a basic understanding of Python programming and trading concepts. You will also need to have access to historical market data from the exchange you are interested in trading on. Most exchanges provide APIs that allow you to access historical market data, which you can use to create custom indicators.

One popular library used for creating custom indicators in trading with Python is the TA-Lib library. TA-Lib is a powerful technical analysis library that provides a wide range of functions for creating custom indicators. To use TA-Lib, you will need to install the library using pip:

214

```python
pip install TA-Lib
```

Once you have installed TA-Lib, you can start creating custom indicators for exchanges in trading. Let's take a look at an example of how to create a simple moving average indicator using Python scripts:

```python
import talib
import numpy as np

# Load historical market data
# Replace this with actual market data from the exchange
close_price = np.array([10, 20, 30, 40, 50, 60, 70, 80, 90, 100])

# Calculate the simple moving average
sma = talib.SMA(close_price, timeperiod=5)

print(sma)
```

In this example, we first import the TA-Lib library and numpy library. We then load historical market data into an array called close_price. Next, we calculate the simple moving average using the talib.SMA function with a time period of 5. Finally, we print the simple moving average values.

Custom indicators can be used to create trading strategies and make informed decisions in the market. By creating custom indicators using Python scripts, traders can gain a deeper understanding of market trends and patterns, which can help them make more profitable trades.

In addition to simple moving averages, there are many other custom indicators that can be created using Python scripts. Some popular custom indicators include exponential moving averages, Bollinger Bands, Relative Strength Index (RSI), and MACD (Moving Average Convergence Divergence).

Here is an example of how to create a Bollinger Bands indicator using Python scripts:

```python
import talib
import numpy as np

# Load historical market data
# Replace this with actual market data from the exchange
close_price = np.array([10, 20, 30, 40, 50, 60, 70, 80, 90, 100])

# Calculate the Bollinger Bands
upper_band, middle_band, lower_band = talib.BBANDS(close_price, timeperiod=5)

print(upper_band, middle_band, lower_band)
```

In this example, we calculate the Bollinger Bands using the talib.BBANDS function with a time period of 5. The Bollinger Bands consist of an upper band, a middle band, and a lower band, which can be used to identify overbought and oversold conditions in the market.

Custom indicators can be used in conjunction with trading strategies to improve trading performance and profitability. By creating custom indicators using Python scripts, traders can automate the process of analyzing market data and making trading decisions.

Creating custom indicators for exchanges in trading using Python scripts is a powerful tool that can help traders gain a deeper understanding of market trends and patterns. By using libraries like TA-Lib, traders can create a wide range of custom indicators to suit their trading strategies and preferences. Custom indicators can be used to create profitable trading strategies and make informed decisions in the market.

Python's simplicity and flexibility make it an ideal language for creating custom indicators in trading.

Implementing Custom Indicators in Python scripts

Implementing custom indicators in Python scripts can be a powerful way to enhance the functionality of your rt trading strategies. By creating your own indicators, you can tailor them to your specific trading style and preferences, giving you a competitive edge in the market. In this article, we will explore how to implement custom indicators in Python scripts, using examples and code snippets to illustrate the process.

To begin, it is important to understand what indicators are and how they can be used in trading. Indicators are mathematical calculations based on historical price data, which are used to analyze and predict future price movements. There are many different types of indicators, such as moving averages, oscillators, and trend lines, each serving a specific purpose in technical analysis.

While there are many pre-built indicators available in popular trading platforms, creating custom indicators can offer a unique advantage. Custom indicators can be tailored to your specific trading strategy, allowing you to incorporate your own unique insights and preferences into your analysis. By creating custom indicators, you can gain a deeper understanding of the market and make more informed trading decisions.

To implement custom indicators in Python scripts, you will need to use a programming library such as Pandas or NumPy to manipulate and analyze data. You will also

218

need to have a basic understanding of Python programming, as well as knowledge of technical analysis concepts. In this example, we will create a simple custom indicator using Python code.

Let's start by defining our custom indicator. For this example, we will create a moving average crossover indicator, which will signal buy or sell opportunities based on the crossover of two moving averages. To create this indicator, we will need to calculate two moving averages - a short-term moving average and a long-term moving average - and then compare their values to generate buy or sell signals.

First, we will import the necessary libraries and define our custom indicator function:

```python
import pandas as pd

def    moving_average_crossover(data,    short_window, long_window):
signals = pd.DataFrame(index=data.index)signals['signal'] = 0.0

# Calculate short-term moving average
signals['short_mavg']                        =
data['Close'].rolling(window=short_window, min_periods=1,   center=False).mean()

# Calculate long-term moving average
signals['long_mavg']                         =
data['Close'].rolling(window=long_window,    min_periods=1,
```

```python
center=False).mean()

    # Generate buy signals
    signals['signal'][short_window:]                        =
np.where(signals['short_mavg'][short_window:]               >
signals['long_mavg'][short_window:], 1.0, 0.0)

    # Generate sell signals

    signals['signal'][short_window:]                        =
np.where(signals['short_mavg'][short_window:]               <
signals['long_mavg'][short_window:], -1.0, 0.0)

    return signals
```

In this function, we first create a DataFrame to store our signals. We then calculate the short-term and long-term moving averages using the `rolling` method in Pandas. Finally, we generate buy and sell signals based on the crossover of the two moving averages.

Next, we will load historical price data into a DataFrame and apply our custom indicator function to generate buy and sell signals:

```python
data = pd.read_csv('historical_data.csv', index_col='Date',
parse_dates=True)short_window = 40
long_window = 100

signals   =   moving_average_crossover(data,   short_window,
```

```
long_window)
```

In this code snippet, we load historical price data from a CSV file into a DataFrame and specify the parameters for our moving average crossover indicator. We then apply the `moving_average_crossover` function to the data to generate buy and sell signals.

Finally, we can visualize the buy and sell signals on a price chart to assess the effectiveness of our custom indicator:

```python
import matplotlib.pyplot as plt

plt.figure(figsize=(10,     6))      plt.plot(data['Close'],
label='Close Price')
plt.plot(signals['short_mavg'],    label='Short-term    Moving
Average')    plt.plot(signals['long_mavg'],     label='Long-term
Moving  Average')

# Plot buy signals
plt.plot(signals.loc[signals['signal']       ==       1.0].index,
signals['short_mavg'][signals['signal']     ==     1.0],    '^',
markersize=10, color='g', lw=0, label='Buy Signal')

# Plot sell signals
plt.plot(signals.loc[signals['signal']       ==      -1.0].index,
signals['short_mavg'][signals['signal']    ==    -1.0],    'v',
markersize=10, color='r', lw=0, label='Sell Signal')

plt.title('Moving Average Crossover Indicator')plt.legend()
plt.show()
```

Chapter 20: Integrating Trading Bots with Exchanges

In today's fast-paced world of trading, automated trading bots have become an essential tool for traders looking to maximize their profits and minimize their risks. These bots are designed to execute trades on behalf of the trader, using predefined algorithms and parameters to make decisions in real-time. However, in order for these bots to be effective, they must be integrated with exchanges in order to have access to real-time market data and execute trades.

Integrating trading bots with exchanges can be a complex process, as each exchange has its own API and requirements for connecting with external systems. In this chapter, we will explore the various steps involved in integrating trading bots with exchanges, as well as some best practices for ensuring a successful integration.

The first step in integrating a trading bot with an exchange is to create an account with the exchange and obtain the necessary API keys. These keys are used to authenticate the bot with the exchange and allow it to access market data and execute trades on behalf of the trader. It is important to keep these keys secure, as they provide access to the trader's account and funds.

Once the API keys have been obtained, the next step is to connect the bot to the exchange's API. This typically involves writing code that communicates with the exchange's servers, sending requests for market data and trade execution. Each exchange has its own API documentation that outlines the various endpoints and parameters that can be used to interact with the exchange's system.

After the bot has been connected to the exchange's API, the next step is to implement the trading strategy that the bot will use to make decisions. This strategy will typically involve a combination of technical indicators, price action analysis, and risk management rules that dictate when to enter and exit trades. The bot will continuously monitor market conditions and execute trades based on the predefined strategy.

One of the key challenges in integrating trading bots with exchanges is ensuring that the bot can handle the high volume of data and execute trades in a timely manner. This requires a robust infrastructure that can support the processing power and network bandwidth required to communicate with the exchange's servers. It is important to monitor the bot's performance and make adjustments as needed to ensure that it can keep up with the fast-paced nature of the markets.

Another important consideration when integrating trading bots with exchanges is the security of the bot and the trader's funds. It is essential to implement proper security measures, such as encryption and authentication, to protect the bot from unauthorized access and ensure that trades are executed securely. Additionally, it is important to regularly audit the bot's code and infrastructure to identify and address any vulnerabilities that could compromise its security.

In conclusion, integrating trading bots with exchanges is a complex process that requires careful planning and implementation. By following the steps outlined in this chapter and adhering to best practices for security and performance, traders can successfully integrate their bots with exchanges and take advantage of the benefits of automated trading. With the right tools and strategies in place, traders can maximize their profits and minimize their risks in today's competitive trading environment.

API Integration with Exchanges with python - scripts

API integration with exchanges is a crucial aspect of automated trading in the cryptocurrency market. By connecting your trading bot or algorithm to exchange APIs, you can access real-time market data, execute trades, and manage your portfolio more efficiently. In this article, we will explore how to integrate APIs with exchanges using Python scripts as examples.

Exchanges provide APIs (Application Programming Interfaces) that allow developers to interact with their trading platforms programmatically. These APIs typically provide endpoints for accessing market data, placing orders, and managing accounts. By leveraging these APIs, you can build custom trading strategies and automate your trading activities.

Python is a popular programming language for building trading bots and algorithms due to its simplicity, versatility, and extensive library support. In this article, we will use Python to demonstrate how to integrate with exchange APIs and perform basic trading operations.

To get started with API integration, you will first need to create an account on the exchange of your choice and generate API keys. API keys consist of a public key and a secret key, which are used to authenticate your requests to the exchange's API. It is essential to keep your API keys secure and not share them with anyone else.

Once you have your API keys, you can start integrating with the exchange's API using Python. In this example, we will use the popular exchange Binance, which provides a comprehensive API for accessing market data and executing trades.

To interact with Binance's API in Python, we can use the `requests` library, which allows us to make HTTP requests to the API endpoints. First, we need to install the `requests` library by running the following command:

```
pip install requests
```

Next, we can create a Python script to interact with Binance's API. Here is an example script that retrieves the current price of Bitcoin (BTC) in USDT from Binance:

```python
import requests

API_KEY = 'your_api_key'
API_SECRET = 'your_api_secret'

url = 'https://api.binance.com/api/v3/ticker/price'
params = {
'symbol': 'BTCUSDT'
}

headers = {
'X-MBX-APIKEY': API_KEY
```

```
}

response    =    requests.get(url,    params=params,
headers=headers)data = response.json()

print(f"The current price of Bitcoin is {data['price']}
USDT")
```
```

In this script, we first define our API key and secret key,
which are used to authenticate our requests to Binance's
API. We then specify the URL of the API endpoint we want
to access, which in this case is the tickerprice endpoint for
the BTCUSDT trading pair.

We also provide the API key in the headers of the HTTP
request to authenticate our request. We then make aGET
request to the API endpoint with the specified parameters
and headers. The response from the API is in JSON
format, which we can parse to extract the current price of
Bitcoin in USDT.

By running this script, we can retrieve the current price of
Bitcoin from Binance's API and display it in the console.
This is just a basic example of how to interact with an
exchange's API using Python. You can expand onthis script
to perform more advanced trading operations, such as
placing orders or managing your portfolio.

API integration with exchanges opens up a world of
possibilities for automated trading and algorithmic trading
strategies. By leveraging exchange APIs with Python
scripts, you can build powerful trading bots that can
```

execute trades based on predefined criteria, analyze market data in real-time, and optimize your trading performance.

In addition to Binance, there are many other exchanges that provide APIs for developers to integrate with, such as Coinbase, Kraken, and Bitfinex. Each exchange has its API documentation, which outlines the available endpoints, parameters, and authentication methods.

When integrating with exchange APIs, it is essential to follow best practices for API security and rate limiting to avoid potential security risks and ensure the stability of your trading bot. Always keep your API keys secure and avoid making too many requests to the API in a short period, as this may result in your requests being throttled or blocked.

API integration with exchanges using Python scripts is a powerful tool for automating your trading activities and gaining a competitive edge in the cryptocurrency market. By leveraging exchange APIs, you can access real-time market data, execute trades, and manage your portfolio more efficiently. With the right skills and knowledge, you can build sophisticated trading bots that can help you achieve your trading goals and maximize your profits.

Automating Trading Processes with python - scripts

Automating trading processes with Python scripts is a powerful way to streamline your trading strategies and increase efficiency. By using Python, a versatile and easy-to-learn programming language, you can automate various aspects of your trading workflow, from data analysis to order execution.

Python is a popular choice for automating trading processes due to its simplicity, flexibility, and extensive libraries for data analysis and visualization. With Python, you can easily access and manipulate financial data, create complex trading algorithms, and execute trades automatically based on predefined criteria.

In this article, we will provide an overview of how to automate trading processes with Python scripts, including examples of common tasks such as data retrieval, analysis, and order execution.

Data Retrieval

One of the first steps in automating trading processes with Python is to retrieve financial data from various sources such as APIs, databases, or web scraping. Python provides several libraries for retrieving data, such as Pandas, Requests, and BeautifulSoup.

For example, you can use the Requests library to retrieve data from a web API such as Alpha Vantage, which provides free access to historical stock prices. Here's an example code snippet that retrieves historical stock prices for a specific symbol using Alpha Vantage API:

```python
import requests

symbol = 'AAPL'
api_key = 'YOUR_API_KEY'

url = f'https://www.alphavantage.co/query?function=TIME_SERIES_DAILY&symbol={symbol}&apikey={api_key}'

response = requests.get(url)data = response.json()

print(data)
```

This code snippet sends a request to the Alpha Vantage API to retrieve daily stock price data for Apple (AAPL) and prints the response in JSON format.

Data Analysis

Once you have retrieved financial data, you can perform various data analysis tasks to gain insights into market trends and patterns. Python provides powerful libraries for data analysis, such as NumPy, Pandas, and Matplotlib.

For example, you can use Pandas to calculate moving averages for stock prices and plot them using Matplotlib.

Here's an example code snippet that calculates a simple moving average for a stock price series:

```python
import pandas as pd
import matplotlib.pyplot as plt

# Load stock price data into a Pandas DataFramedata =
pd.read_csv('stock_prices.csv')

# Calculate 50-day simple moving average
data['SMA_50'] = data['Close'].rolling(window=50).mean()

# Plot stock prices and moving average
plt.figure(figsize=(12, 6)) plt.plot(data['Close'],
label='Stock Price') plt.plot(data['SMA_50'], label='50-
day SMA')plt.legend()
plt.show()
```

This code snippet loads stock price data from a CSV file, calculates a 50-day simple moving average, and plotsthe stock prices along with the moving average using Matplotlib.

Order Execution

Once you have analyzed financial data and developed trading strategies, you can automate order execution using Python scripts. Python provides libraries for connecting to trading platforms and executing orders programmatically, such as Alpaca Trade API, Interactive Brokers API, and MetaTrader API.

For example, you can use the Alpaca Trade API to execute market orders for a specific stock. Here's an examplecode snippet that submits a market order to buy 100 shares of Apple (AAPL) using Alpaca Trade API:

```python
import alpaca_trade_api as tradeapi

api_key = 'YOUR_API_KEY' api_secret = 'YOUR_API_SECRET'
base_url = 'https://paper-api.alpaca.markets'
api = tradeapi.REST(api_key, api_secret, base_url, api_version='v2')symbol = 'AAPL'
quantity = 100

api.submit_order(symbol=symbol,
```

```
qty=quantity,              side='buy',              type='market',
time_in_force='gtc'
)
```
```

This code snippet connects to the Alpaca Trade API using your API key and secret, submits a market order to buy 100 shares of Apple (AAPL), and sets the order to remain active until filled.

Conclusion

Automating trading processes with Python scripts can help you streamline your trading strategies, increase efficiency, and reduce manual errors. By leveraging Python's powerful libraries for data analysis, visualization, and order execution, you can develop sophisticated trading algorithms and execute trades automatically based on predefined criteria.

We provided an overview of how to automate trading processes with Python scripts, including examples of common tasks such as data retrieval, analysis, and order execution. By following these examples and exploring Python's extensive libraries and APIs, you can take your trading automation to the next level and stay ahead of the competition in the fast-paced world of financial markets.
```

Chapter 21: Trading Psychology and Discipline

Trading in the financial markets can be a highly rewarding but also challenging endeavor. Success in trading is not just about having a good strategy or understanding market dynamics; it also requires a strong grasp of trading psychology and discipline. In this chapter, we will explore the importance of trading psychology and discipline in achieving success in the markets.

Trading Psychology

Trading psychology refers to the mental and emotional factors that influence a trader's decision-making process. It is crucial to understand that trading is not just about analyzing charts and making predictions; it also involves managing emotions such as fear, greed, and anxiety. These emotions can often cloud judgment and lead to poor decision-making, which can result in significant losses.

One of the key psychological challenges that traders face is dealing with losses. It is natural to feel disappointed or frustrated when a trade does not go as planned, but it is essential to remain calm and objective in such situations. Dwelling on losses or letting emotions dictate trading decisions can lead to a downward spiral of more losses and increased emotional distress.

Another common psychological challenge for traders is the fear of missing out (FOMO). This fear can lead to impulsive trading decisions based on the fear of missing out on potential profits. It is important to remember that the markets will always present new opportunities, and it is better to miss out on a trade than to enter a position hastily and regret it later.

Greed is another emotion that can negatively impact trading performance. Traders may become overly focused on making profits and take unnecessary risks to achieve their financial goals. It is essential to set realistic expectations and stick to a trading plan to avoid falling into the trap of greed.

Discipline

Discipline is a crucial aspect of successful trading. It involves following a set of rules and guidelines consistently, even when faced with challenging market conditions or emotional turmoil. Discipline helps traders stay focused on their goals and avoid making impulsive decisions that can lead to losses.

One of the key components of trading discipline is having a well-defined trading plan. A trading plan outlines the trader's goals, risk tolerance, entry and exit points, and money management strategies. Following a trading plan helps traders stay organized and focused on their objectives, even in the face of uncertainty.

Risk management is another essential aspect of trading discipline. Traders should never risk more than they can afford to lose on a single trade and should always use stop-loss orders to limit potential losses. By managing risk effectively, traders can protect their capital and avoid significant drawdowns.

Patience is also a crucial element of trading discipline. Markets can be unpredictable, and it is essential to wait for the right opportunities to present themselves before entering a trade. Impulsive trading can lead to unnecessary losses and erode trading capital over time.

Trading psychology and discipline are essential components of successful trading. By understanding and managing emotions such as fear, greed, and impatience, traders can make informed decisions and avoid common pitfalls in the markets.

Discipline helps traders stay focused on their goals and follow a well-defined trading plan, which is crucial for long-term success. By mastering trading psychology and discipline, traders can improve their performance and achieve their financial goals in the markets.

Understanding Trading Psychology

Understanding trading psychology is essential for any trader looking to succeed in the financial markets. While many traders focus solely on technical analysis and market fundamentals, the psychological aspect of trading is often overlooked. However, it plays a crucial role in determining a trader's success or failure.

Trading psychology refers to the emotional and mental state of a trader when making trading decisions. It involves understanding how emotions such as fear, greed, and overconfidence can impact a trader's decision-making process. By being aware of these psychological factors, traders can better control their emotions and make more rational trading decisions.

One of the most common emotions that traders experience is fear. Fear can arise when a trade is not going as planned, causing a trader to panic and make impulsive decisions. This can lead to selling a position prematurely or holding onto a losing trade for too long. Fear can also prevent traders from taking calculated risks that could potentially lead to profitable trades.

Greed is another emotion that can impact a trader's decision-making process. When a trade is going well, a trader may become greedy and hold onto a position for too long in the hopes of making more profit. This can lead to missing out on taking profits at the right time and ultimately losing money. Greed can also cause traders to take on excessive risk in pursuit of higher returns, which can lead to significant losses.

Overconfidence is another psychological factor that can negatively impact a trader's performance. When a trader experiences a string of successful trades, they may become overconfident in their abilities and take on more risk than they should. This can lead to making careless decisions and ultimately losing money. It's important for traders to remain humble and objective, even in the face of success.

To overcome these psychological challenges, traders must develop a disciplined trading plan and stick to it. This includes setting clear trading goals, risk management strategies, and entry and exit points for trades. By having a plan in place, traders can reduce the impact of emotions on their decision-making process and make more rational trading decisions.

Another important aspect of trading psychology is managing stress. The financial markets can be volatile and unpredictable, leading to high levels of stress for traders. It's important for traders to find healthy ways to cope with stress, such as exercise, meditation, or talking to a mentor or therapist. By managing stress effectively, traders can make better decisions and improve their overall performance.

In addition to managing emotions and stress, traders must also develop a mindset of continuous learning and improvement. The financial markets are constantly evolving, and traders must stay informed about market trends, economic indicators, and geopolitical events that can impact their trades. By staying educated and adapting to changing market conditions, traders can increase their chances of success.

It's also important for traders to seek feedback from experienced traders and mentors. By learning from others who have been successful in the markets, traders can gain valuable insights and improve their trading skills. This can help traders avoid common pitfalls and accelerate their learning curve.

Understanding trading psychology is essential for any trader looking to succeed in the financial markets. By being aware of the emotional and mental factors that can impact trading decisions, traders can improve their decision-making process and increase their chances of success.

Techniques for Maintaining Discipline Trading Psychology

Trading in the financial markets can be a highly stressful and emotionally challenging endeavor. The volatility and unpredictability of the markets can often lead to impulsive decision-making and emotional trading, which can result in significant losses. In order to be successful in trading, it is essential to maintain discipline and control over your emotions. This is where trading psychology comes into play.

Trading psychology is the study of how emotions and mental states can affect a trader's decision-making process. It is important to understand that trading is not just about analyzing charts and data, but also about managing your emotions and maintaining discipline. Here are some techniques for maintaining discipline in trading psychology:

Develop a Trading Plan: One of the most important aspects of maintaining discipline in trading is to have a well-defined trading plan. A trading plan outlines your trading strategy, risk management rules, and goals. By having a plan in place, you can avoid making impulsive decisions based on emotions and stick to your trading strategy.

Set Clear Goals: Setting clear and realistic goals is essential for maintaining discipline in trading. By having clear goals, you can stay focused on your trading strategy and avoid getting swayed by emotions. Make sure your goals are specific, measurable, achievable, relevant, and time-bound (SMART).

Practice Patience: Patience is a key trait that all successful traders possess. It is important to be patient andwait for the right trading opportunities to present themselves. Avoid rushing into trades out of fear of missingout or greed. Remember, it is better to miss a trade than to enter a bad trade.

Manage Your Emotions: Emotions such as fear, greed, and overconfidence can have a significant impact on your trading decisions. It is important to be aware of your emotions and how they can influence your trading. Develop strategies to manage your emotions, such as taking breaks, practicing mindfulness, or using relaxation techniques.

Follow Your Trading Rules: It is important to have a set of trading rules that you follow consistently. These rules should include entry and exit criteria, risk management guidelines, and position sizing rules. By following your trading rules, you can avoid making impulsive decisions based on emotions.

Keep a Trading Journal: Keeping a trading journal can help you track your trades, analyze your performance, and identify areas for improvement. By reviewing your trading journal regularly, you can learn from your mistakes, identify patterns in your trading behavior, and make adjustments to your trading strategy.

Practice Risk Management: Risk management is a crucial

aspect of maintaining discipline in trading. By managing your risk effectively, you can protect your capital and avoid large losses. Make sure to use stop-loss orders, diversify your trades, and only risk a small percentage of your capital on each trade.

Stay Disciplined: Discipline is the key to success in trading. It is important to stick to your trading plan, follow your rules, and avoid making emotional decisions. Remember that trading is a marathon, not a sprint, and consistency is key to long-term success.

Maintaining discipline in trading psychology is essential for success in the financial markets. By developing a trading plan, setting clear goals, practicing patience, managing your emotions, following your trading rules, keeping a trading journal, practicing risk management, and staying disciplined, you can improve your trading performance and achieve your financial goals. Remember that trading psychology is just as important as technical analysis and fundamental research in trading, and by mastering your emotions, you can become a more successful trader.

Chapter 22: Real-Time Data Processing and Analysis

In today's fast-paced digital world, the ability to process and analyze data in real-time is crucial for businesses to stay competitive and make informed decisions. Real-time data processing and analysis allow organizations to quickly respond to changing market conditions, customer needs, and other external factors that can impact their operations. In this chapter, we will explore the importance of real-time data processing and analysis, the challenges associated with it, and the technologies and techniques that can help organizations effectively manage and analyze data in real-time.

Importance of Real-Time Data Processing and Analysis

Real-time data processing and analysis enable organizations to make timely and informed decisions based on up-to-date information. By processing and analyzing data in real-time, businesses can identify trends, patterns, and anomalies as they happen, allowing them to take immediate action to capitalize on opportunities or mitigate risks. Real-time data processing also enables organizations to monitor and track key performance indicators (KPIs) in real-time, providing them with valuable insights into their operations and helping them make data-driven decisions.

Real-time data processing and analysis are particularly important in industries such as finance, healthcare, retail, and manufacturing, where even a slight delay in data processing can have significant consequences. For example,in the finance industry, real-time data processing is essential for monitoring stock prices, detecting fraudulent transactions, and executing trades at the right time.

 In healthcare, real-time data processing can help doctors and nurses make faster and more accurate diagnoses, leading to better patient outcomes. In retail, real-time data processing can help companies optimize their inventory management, pricing strategies, and marketing campaigns to meet customer demand and increase sales.

Challenges of Real-Time Data Processing and Analysis

While real-time data processing and analysis offer numerous benefits, they also present several challenges that organizations must overcome. One of the main challenges is the sheer volume of data that needs to be processed in real-time. With the proliferation of IoT devices, social media platforms, and other sources of real-time data, organizations are inundated with vast amounts of data that must be processed quickly and accurately.

Another challenge is the need for high-speed data processing and analysis capabilities. Traditional data processing systems are often not equipped to handle the speed and volume of real-time data, leading to delaysand bottlenecks in data processing. Organizations must invest in advanced technologies such as in-memory computing, stream processing, and distributed computing to process and analyze data in real-time efficiently.

Security and privacy concerns are also significant challenges in real-time data processing and analysis. With the increasing amount of sensitive data being processed in real-time, organizations must ensure that their data processing systems are secure and comply with data protection regulations. This requires implementing robust security measures such as encryption, access controls, and data masking to protect data from unauthorized access and breaches.

Technologies and Techniques for Real-Time Data Processing and Analysis To overcome the challenges of real-time data processing and analysis, organizations can leverage a variety of technologies and techniques that enable them to process and analyze data quickly and accurately.

One such technology is in-memory computing, which allows organizations to store and process data in memory rather than on disk, enabling faster data processing speeds. In-memory computing is particularly well-suited for real-time data processing applications that require low latency and high throughput.

Another technology that organizations can use for real-time data processing and analysis is stream processing. Stream processing enables organizations to process data continuously as it is generated, allowing them to analyze and act on data in real-time. Stream processing platforms such as Apache Kafka, Apache Flink, and Apache Storm provide organizations with the ability to process and analyze data streams from various sources, including IoT devices, social media platforms, and sensors.

Distributed computing is another key technology for real-time data processing and analysis. Distributed computing platforms such as Apache Hadoop and Apache Spark enable organizations to distribute data processing tasks across multiple nodes in a cluster, allowing them to process large volumes of data quickly and efficiently. By leveraging distributed computing, organizations can scale their data processing capabilities to handle the growing volume of real-time data.

In addition to technologies, organizations can also use techniques such as data visualization, machine learning, and predictive analytics to analyze real-time data effectively. Data visualization tools such as Tableau, Power BI, and Qlik enable organizations to visualize and explore data in real-time, making it easier to identify trends, patterns, and outliers. Machine learning algorithms can be used to analyze real-time data and make predictions based on historical data, enabling organizations to anticipate future trends and take proactive actions.

Real-time data processing and analysis are essential for organizations to stay competitive and make informed decisions in today's fast-paced digital world. By processing and analyzing data in real-time, organizations can identify trends, patterns, and anomalies as they happen, enabling them to respond quickly to changing market conditions, customer needs, and other external factors.

Handling Real-Time Data in Python - scripts

Real-time data handling is a critical aspect of many applications, especially those that deal with streaming data or need to respond quickly to changing information. In Python, there are several libraries and techniques that can be used to effectively handle real-time data. In this article, we will explore some examples of how to handle real-time data in Python using scripts.

One of the most common ways to handle real-time data in Python is by using the `requests` library to make HTTP requests to an API that provides real-time data. For example, let's say we want to retrieve real-time stock prices from a financial API. We can use the following script to make a request to the API and print out the latest stock price:

```python
import requests

url = 'https://api.example.com/stocks'
response = requests.get(url)

if response.status_code == 200:
    data = response.json()
    latest_price = data['price']
    print(f'The latest stock price is: {latest_price}')
else:
    print('Failed to retrieve data')
```

In this script, we first import the `requests` library and then define the URL of the API we want to make a request to. We then use the `requests.get()` method to make a

GET request to the API and store the response in the `response` variable. We check if the status code of the response is 200, which indicates a successful request, and then extract the latest stock price from the JSON data returned by the API.

Another common way to handle real-time data in Python is by using the `websocket-client` library to connect to a WebSocket server that streams real-time data. For example, let's say we want to connect to a WebSocket server that streams live cryptocurrency prices. We can use the following script to connect to the WebSocket server and print out the latest price updates:

```python
import websocket

def on_message(ws, message): print(f'Received message: {message}')

def on_error(ws, error):print(f'Error: {error}')

def on_close(ws, close_status_code, close_msg): print('Connection closed')
```

```python
def on_open(ws):
    print('Connection opened')

if __name__ == '__main__':
    ws = websocket.WebSocketApp('wss://api.example.com/cryptocurrency',on_message=on_message,
    on_error=on_error,                on_close=on_close,
    on_open=on_open) ws.run_forever()
```

In this script, we first import the `websocket` library and then define several callback functions that will be called when certain events occur, such as receiving a message, encountering an error, closing the connection, or opening the connection. We then create a `WebSocketApp` object with the URL of the WebSocket server and the callback functions, and call the `run_forever()` method to start listening for messages from the server.

Real-time data handling in Python can also involve processing and analyzing data as it is received. For example,let's say we want to calculate the moving average of a stream of stock prices in real-time. We can use the following script to connect to a WebSocket server that streams live stock prices and calculate the moving average as new prices are received:

```python
import websocket import numpy as np

prices = []
```

```python
def on_message(ws, message):
price = float(message)prices.append(price)
moving_average = np.mean(prices[-10:]) print(f'Moving average: {moving_average}')

def on_error(ws, error):
print(f'Error: {error}')

def on_close(ws, close_status_code, close_msg):
print('Connection closed')

def on_open(ws):
print('Connection opened')

if____name_== '__main_':
ws                                                                =
websocket.WebSocketApp('wss://api.example.com/stocks'
,on_message=on_message,
```

```
on_error=on_error,                    on_close=on_close,
on_open=on_open) ws.run_forever()
```

In this script, we maintain a list of stock prices in the `prices` variable and calculate the moving average of the last 10 prices using the `numpy` library. Whenever a new price is received, we append it to the `prices` list and calculate the moving average of the last 10 prices. We then print out the moving average to the console.

Handling real-time data in Python involves making requests to APIs, connecting to WebSocket servers, and processing and analyzing data as it is received. By using libraries such as `requests`, `websocket- client`, and `numpy`, we can effectively handle real-time data in Python and build applications that respond quickly to changing information.

The examples provided in this article demonstrate how to handle real-time data in Python using scripts, but there are many other techniques and libraries available for real-time data handling in Python.

Analyzing Real-Time Market Trends with python - scripts

Analyzing real-time market trends is essential for making informed decisions in the fast-paced world of trading and investing. With the help of Python scripts, you can automate the process of collecting, analyzing, and visualizing market data in real-time, giving you a competitive edge in the financial markets.

Python is a versatile programming language that is widely used in data analysis, machine learning, and web development. It has a rich ecosystem of libraries and tools that make it easy to work with financial data and build sophisticated trading algorithms.

Step 1: Installing the necessary libraries

Before we can start analyzing real-time market trends, we need to install the necessary libraries. You can install pandas, matplotlib, and requests using pip, the Python package manager.

```
```

pip install pandas matplotlib requests
```
```

Step 2: Collecting real-time market data

To collect real-time market data, we will use the Alpha Vantage API, which provides free access to historical and real-time market data. You will need to sign up for an API key on the Alpha Vantage website to access the data.

```python
import requests

API_KEY = "YOUR_API_KEY"
SYMBOL = "AAPL"

url = f'https://www.alphavantage.co/query?function=TIME_SERIES_INTRADAY&symbol={SYMBOL}&interval=1min&apikey={API_KEY}"

response = requests.get(url)
data = response.json()

print(data)
```

This code snippet sends a request to the Alpha Vantage API to retrieve real-time intraday data for the Apple stock (AAPL) at a one-minute interval. The data is returned in JSON format, which we can parse and analyze using Python.

Step 3: Analyzing real-time market trends

Now that we have collected real-time market data, we can analyze it to identify trends and patterns. We will use the pandas library to load the data into a DataFrame and calculate some basic statistics.

```python
import pandas as pd

df = pd.DataFrame(data['Time Series (1min)']).T df = df.astype(float)

print(df.head()) print(df.describe())
```

This code snippet loads the real-time market data into a pandas DataFrame and converts the data types to float for numerical analysis. We then print the first few rows of the DataFrame and some basic statistics such as mean, median, and standard deviation.

Step 4: Visualizing real-time market trends

To visualize real-time market trends, we will use the matplotlib library to create interactive plots that update in real-time as new data comes in. We will plot the closing prices of the Apple stock over time.

```python
import matplotlib.pyplot as plt
import matplotlib.animation as animation
```

```
fig, ax = plt.subplots()x = []
y = []

def animate(i):
x.append(i)
y.append(df['4. close'].iloc[-1])ax.clear()
ax.plot(x, y)
ax.set_title('Real-Time          Market          Trends')
ax.set_xlabel('Time') ax.set_ylabel('Closing Price')

ani    =    animation.FuncAnimation(fig,    animate,
interval=60000)plt.show()
```
```

This code snippet creates an animated plot that updates
every minute with the latest closing price of the Apple
```

stock. The x-axis represents time, while the y-axis represents the closing price. You can customize the plot by adding additional data points or changing the plot style.

Analyzing real-time market trends with Python scripts can give you valuable insights into the financial markets and help you make better trading and investment decisions. By automating the process of collecting, analyzing, and visualizing market data, you can stay ahead of the competition and capitalize on emerging trends.

In this article, we walked you through an example of how to analyze real-time market trends using Python scripts. We used the pandas, matplotlib, and requests libraries to collect, analyze, and visualize real-time market data for the Apple stock. You can apply the same principles to analyze other stocks, cryptocurrencies, or financial instruments.

Remember to always use caution when trading or investing in the financial markets and do your own research before making any decisions. Python scripts are a powerful tool for analyzing real-time market trends, but they should be used in conjunction with other sources of information and analysis.

Conclusion

As we reach the end of *Python for Cryptocurrency Trading: Navigate the Digital Currency Market*, it's clear that the world of digital currencies is as thrilling as it is unpredictable. Throughout this book, we have delved deep into the complexities of the cryptocurrency market, arming you with the knowledge and tools to not just survive, but thrive in this digital gold rush.

We began our journey by exploring the fundamentals of cryptocurrencies and the underlying technology of blockchain. Understanding these core concepts is crucial, as they form the bedrock upon which all successful trading strategies are built. From there, we ventured into the realm of Python programming, harnessing its power to create sophisticated trading bots that can execute trades with precision and speed that human traders can only dream of.

Analyzing blockchain data was another critical focus, providing you with the skills to glean valuable insights from the vast sea of information embedded in every transaction. This ability to decode the data gives you a significant edge, enabling you to make informed decisions based on real-time market movements and trends.

But knowledge alone is not enough. This book also emphasized the importance of implementing effective trading strategies tailored to the volatile nature of cryptocurrencies. We discussed various approaches, from algorithmic trading to leveraging machine learning models, all designed to maximize your profitability while managing risk.

The main takeaway from this journey is clear: mastering cryptocurrency trading with Python is not just about understanding the technology or the market. It's about combining these elements to develop strategies that are both innovative and effective. By doing so, you position yourself to capitalize on the immense opportunities this market offers, while navigating its inherent risks with confidence and skill.

As you close this book, remember that the world of cryptocurrency trading is constantly evolving. Stay curious, keep learning, and continue refining your strategies. The tools and insights you've gained here are just the beginning. Use them as a foundation to build your trading prowess and to carve out your success in the dynamic landscape of digital currencies.

Biography

J.P. Morgan is a passionate advocate for the transformative power of technology and finance. With a deep-seated expertise in Python programming, finance, and web development, Morgan has spent years navigating the intricate world of cryptocurrency trading. His extensive experience and relentless curiosity have made him a sought-after authority in the field, dedicated to demystifying complex financial concepts and making them accessible to all.

Morgan's journey began with a fascination for coding, which quickly evolved into a love for Python due to its versatility and power. This passion seamlessly blended with his interest in finance, leading him to explore the dynamic and often unpredictable realm of cryptocurrencies. Over the years, he has developed and refined numerous trading strategies, leveraging his programming skills to create innovative trading bots and analytical tools that provide a significant edge in the volatile digital currency market.

When he's not immersed in the world of finance and coding, J.P. Morgan enjoys exploring the latest trends in web development, constantly seeking new ways to integrate cutting-edge technologies into his work. His enthusiasm for continuous learning and innovation is matched only by his commitment to sharing his knowledge with others.

Through his writing, he aims to empower readers to

harness the potential of Python and cryptocurrency trading, equipping them with the skills and confidence to succeed in this exciting field.

Beyond his professional pursuits, Morgan is an avid traveler and a tech enthusiast who loves staying ahead of the curve in the ever-evolving landscape of digital technology. His vibrant personality and unwavering dedication to his craft make him not just a knowledgeable expert, but a truly inspiring figure in the world of finance and technology.

Glossary: Python for Cryptocurrency Trading

Python is a high-level, interpreted programming language that is widely used in the field of cryptocurrency trading. It is known for its simplicity and readability, making it an ideal choice for beginners and experienced programmers alike. In this glossary, we will explore some of the key terms and concepts related to using Python for cryptocurrency trading.

Algorithmic Trading: Algorithmic trading is a method of executing trades using pre-defined instructions based on mathematical models and algorithms. Python is commonly used for algorithmic trading in the cryptocurrency market due to its flexibility and ease of use.

API (Application Programming Interface): An API is a set of rules and protocols that allow different software applications to communicate with each other. Cryptocurrency exchanges typically provide APIs that allow traders to access market data, place orders, and manage their accounts programmatically using Python.

Backtesting: Backtesting is the process of testing a trading strategy using historical market data to evaluate its performance. Python libraries such as Pandas and Matplotlib are commonly used for backtesting cryptocurrency trading strategies.

Candlestick Chart: A candlestick chart is a type of

financial chart used to represent price movements in a particular time frame. Python libraries such as Plotly and Matplotlib can be used to create candlestick charts for analyzing cryptocurrency price trends.

Cryptocurrency: A cryptocurrency is a digital or virtual currency that uses cryptography for security and operates independently of a central authority. Examples of popular cryptocurrencies include Bitcoin, Ethereum, and Litecoin.

Exchange: A cryptocurrency exchange is a platform where traders can buy, sell, and exchange cryptocurrencies. Python can be used to interact with exchange APIs to automate trading strategies and manage cryptocurrency portfolios.

Machine Learning: Machine learning is a branch of artificial intelligence that uses algorithms to analyze and interpret data, make predictions, and automate decision-making processes. Python libraries such as Scikit-learn and TensorFlow can be used for machine learning in cryptocurrency trading.

Order Book: An order book is a list of buy and sell orders for a particular cryptocurrency on an exchange. Python scripts can be used to retrieve and analyze order book data to identify trading opportunities and make informed decisions.

Risk Management: Risk management is the process of identifying, assessing, and mitigating risks in cryptocurrency trading. Python can be used to calculate risk metrics, such as volatility and Sharpe ratio, to optimize trading strategies and protect against potential losses.

Technical Analysis: Technical analysis is a method of evaluating securities based on historical price and volume data to predict future price movements. Python libraries such as TA-Lib and Plotly can be used to perform technical analysis on cryptocurrency price charts.

Trading Bot: A trading bot is a software program that automatically executes trades on behalf of a trader based on pre-defined rules and strategies. Python is commonly used to develop trading bots for cryptocurrency markets due to its versatility and extensive library support.

Wallet: A cryptocurrency wallet is a digital tool that allows users to store, send, and receive cryptocurrencies securely. Python can be used to interact with wallet APIs to manage cryptocurrency balances and transactions.

Web Scraping: Web scraping is the process of extracting data from websites using automated tools. Python libraries such as BeautifulSoup and Scrapy can be used to scrape cryptocurrency market data, news, and social media sentiment for analysis and trading purposes.

Arbitrage: Arbitrage is the practice of buying and selling assets simultaneously on different markets to profit from price discrepancies. Python scripts can be used to identify arbitrage opportunities in cryptocurrency exchanges and execute trades quickly to capitalize on price differentials.

Cryptocurrency Market Data: Cryptocurrency market data

includes real-time price quotes, trading volumes, order book data, and historical price charts for various cryptocurrencies. Python libraries such as ccxt and Cryptocompare can be used to access and analyze cryptocurrency market data for trading purposes.

Portfolio Management: Portfolio management is the process of selecting and managing a diversified portfolio of investments to achieve specific financial goals. Python can be used to track cryptocurrency holdings, calculate portfolio performance, and rebalance asset allocations based on market conditions.

Quantitative Analysis: Quantitative analysis is the use of mathematical and statistical methods to analyze financial data and make informed trading decisions. Python libraries such as NumPy and SciPy can be used for quantitative analysis in cryptocurrency trading to identify patterns, trends, and correlations in market data.

Scalping: Scalping is a trading strategy that involves making small profits from frequent trades on short-term price movements. Python scripts can be used to automate scalping strategies in cryptocurrency markets by placing high-frequency trades and capturing small price differentials.

Sentiment Analysis: Sentiment analysis is the process of analyzing text data, such as social media posts and news articles, to gauge public sentiment and market sentiment towards a particular cryptocurrency.